Of all the living prophets of our mighty God in 2003, Rod Parsley is one who truly drinks from the oldest wells, drinking from the most living, flowing, leaping water of God's everlasting fountains.

To read Rod's books, to hear him speak or to be in his presence is to feel the presence of the living God. It affects me every time.

That's why his newest book stirs the core of my being as it will yours as you plunge into it at once. God speaks in this book. I heard Him speak to me, and I believe you will hear Him, too.

I once asked his mother, "Mrs. Parsley, has your son, Rod, always had this powerful way with words, being able to carry one into the story like he's there himself, feeling and seeing and breathing the power of it?"

She replied. "Since a lad, but more now since each year he grows closer and closer to the Lord Jesus Christ."

Yes, like me, I believe you will find yourself squarely in the middle of this book of Rod Parsley's—unforgettably!

—Oral Roberts, Founder/Chancellor
Oral Roberts University

Rod Parsley's book *Ancient Wells—Living Water* is a call to the church of Jesus Christ to revisit the wells of our salvation; to redig them until they become supernatural sources that refresh and revive us. I encourage you to read this book; you will enjoy it.

—Dr. John C. Hagee, Senior Pastor
Cornerstone Church
John Hagee Ministries

ROD PARSLEY

ANCIENT WELLS LIVING WATER

GOD INVITES YOU TO COME AND DRINK

ANCIENT WELLS—LIVING WATER by Rod Parsley
Published by Charisma House
A part of Strang Communications Company
600 Rinehart Road
Lake Mary, Florida 32746
www.charismahouse.com

Unless otherwise noted, all Scripture quotations are from the King James Version of the Bible.

Scripture quotations marked NIV are from the Holy Bible, New International Version. Copyright © 1973, 1978, 1984, International Bible Society. Used by permission.

Scripture quotations marked NKJV are from the New King James Version of the Bible. Copyright © 1979, 1980, 1982 by Thomas Nelson, Inc., publishers. Used by permission.

Cover design by Eric Powell
Cover illustration by Grace Devito
Interior design by Sallie Traynor

Library of Congress Cataloging-in-Publication Data
Parsley, Rod.
  Ancient wells, living water / Rod Parsley.
     p. cm.
  ISBN 0-88419-942-8
  1. Spiritual life—Christianity. I. Title.
  BV4501.3 3P374 2003
  248.4—dc21
                                        2002152750
03 04 05 06 07 — 8765432
Printed in the United States of America

Contents

Prologue:
The Ancient
Well of Man

I want to tell you a story...

A man from a mighty desert nation once set out to dig a well. He swung his pickax again and again in a furious assault against the stony soil. The sun beat down over the parched land. The man labored, yet the ground seemed unwilling to yield to his violent attack.

Suddenly, the voice of God boomed across the barren wasteland.

"My son," God said to the man, "I am here."

"Who are You?" the man shouted back, barely glancing up as he worked.

"I am the Wellspring of all life. I died in agony that you might live in victory."

"I never asked You to die for me," the man replied with contempt as he kept on digging. "Let me dig my well, that I will have need to draw from no other."

"Take refuge in My wells, and you will never thirst again."

"I want my own source to quench me in these times of drought," the man defiantly yelled back.

"My precious child," the Lord said with compassion, "I am your source of living water. Rely on Me."

The man ignored God.

"Talk with Me," God pleaded, "as a Father with His son."

Silence. The man continued desperately pummeling the rocky earth. One inch. Two. Four.

The clouds darkened.

The sun beat down. Three feet...five feet. The man hewed to the stubborn labor in his pit.

The man's breathing became strained. He stumbled again and again. His hands blistered. His knees buckled.

God brought clouds to shelter the man from the heat.

"Let My waters quench you," the Lord spoke one last time. No response.

The man, ignoring his Creator, toiled onward, deep into the rocky ground. Sweating...heaving...faltering...weakening...breaking.

And God wept.

The man quickened his pace. Six feet. Nine. Twelve. The clouds grew black. Rain dropped. Soon the man realized that he had dug his hole so deep he couldn't get out.

"God, help me!" he called out to God at last. "I have dug myself in too deep!"

Then, the storm. Furious. Vehement. A deluge the man had never before experienced or even imagined. He dropped his pickax and huddled at the muddy bottom of the deep shaft, broken and aged before his time.

"Help me," he begged weakly. "God? Are You still there?"

"I am always here for you," God answered, "waiting for you to reach out to Me."

"Then please, Lord," the man shivered pitifully in the cold, hard rain, his voice barely a whisper, "please...please forgive me for digging my well and ignoring *Yours*."

"I forgive you, My child," replied God gently. "You are My vessel, of My making. It is I who fills you from My endless wells of power, presence and providence. Will you receive from My wells and drink of them alone?" God asked.

"Yes," the man cried tearfully. "I will receive, I will drink, and I will learn from Your wells alone forevermore."

And the man's storm abated, and the rains became sweeping, gentle and warm.

And the sweet rain of God's presence filled up the man's well, and the man rose to the top...and stepped out onto solid ground, alive and refreshed.

"Thank You for freeing me!" the man shouted with joy. "I love You, Father!"

The sky filled and shone with God's bright light and sparkling promise.

The man never doubted God again. And his well never ran dry.

In this book, you too will have an opportunity to draw from God's wells and drink His living water. Ten ancient wells of scriptural doctrine will be presented to you from wells dug by our forefathers. These are wells that Christians today desperately need to redig, as if we are burrowing into the heart of God Himself, so that a spiritual rejuvenation may sweep the land, the well of God in our hearts be filled to overflowing with His power, provision and presence, and we can rediscover His plan for redemption of mankind.

In the pages that follow, join me in rediscovering these incredible, ancient wells, and watch as they become your fountains of spiritual rejuvenation...

No Mere Hole
in the Ground

Chapter **1**

I grew up in Columbus, Ohio, but Kentucky was my real home. Family roots dug deep back in the "hollers," where most young men were destined for dark days in the damp coal mines of eastern Kentucky, toiling in wells of hot soot.

Many men, like my father, traveled north to Ohio, where life held the promise of a brighter future. Thousands of Kentuckians trudged north, filled with hope in the innocent days of the early 1960s.

During my childhood, we would make the trek back to the coal fields nearly every weekend to visit family. My sister Debbie and I were so familiar with the route that we could close our eyes and picture everything passing by, like a

Saturday matinee. Wood-slat boxcars, clickity-clacking. Tall yellow ears of corn, waving. Walgreens Five and Dime, beckoning. Our shiny little faces grinned out the window, eyes screwed shut, Debbie's pigtails flying straight back, my flat-top stiff as a porcupine. If you accidentally opened your mouth and gulped speeding air, it'd nearly choke off your giggles. We were goin' places!

Dad, Mom, Debbie and I would drive from the south side of Columbus, down Route 23 along the Scioto River, tearing across the flatlands of central Ohio, all the way to the gently bending hills of Appalachia. During the long drive, Debbie and I would invent all sorts of games to make the time fly by so we'd suddenly be at Grandma Mimi's. The closer we got to Mimi's house, the greater our anticipation.

Nestled into the side of a mountain, Mimi's modest house was a welcome haven for us. Unlike many people of that time, Mimi was indifferent to modern conveniences. She happily lived where outhouses were more common than indoor bathrooms. Fruits and vegetables were home grown. Cows, chickens and pigs were raised to feed the family. Mimi was a simple woman who lived an uncomplicated life.

There was nothing more thrilling than a visit to Mimi's. But looking out the window from the back seat of that dusty old Ford, my hope was always fixed on something else at Mimi's. The old well...

Wells have brought both blessing and burden.

To me, that old well was one of the most exciting things about Mimi's place. A narrow trail of haggard grass, matted down like worn carpet, led to the well. The well was mysterious and deep, and nearly overgrown with vines and foliage. Mesmerizing noises gurgled from its depths.

With advancements in technology and science over the years, wells like Mimi's are pretty much gone. Nowadays it's a thing of fading memories to tread down a dirt path, turn a crank, dip a cupped hand into a swollen wooden bucket and sip sweet waters from an ancient well.

Mimi knew the secret of that old well. It was no mere hole in the ground. It held a supernatural treasure beyond time…

What's in a Well?

The Bible has much to say about wells:

- It was at Jacob's well where Jesus revealed Himself as the Messiah to a Samaritan woman and offered her new life through His living water. (See John 4:1–30.)

- It was at a well at the pool of Bethesda where an angel troubled the waters, and whoever stepped into the water first was immediately made whole. (See John 5:2–4.)

- It was from a well called the Pool of Gihon (also called the Virgin's Fount) that a stream flowed to the bottom of the Kidron Valley and washed away the blood from the daily sacrifices on the Temple Mount to the Dead Sea. (See 2 Chronicles 33:14.)

- It was at a well in the desert of Beersheba that Hagar and Ishmael were delivered from death. (See Genesis 21:14–21.)

For nations throughout history, wells have brought both blessing and burden. Wells that were the only convenient source of fresh water have been central to the survival or failure of many societies throughout history. Great cultures have flourished when water was pure and plentiful; others have collapsed when the wells ran dry, became polluted or were overtaken by an enemy. Neighbors and nations fought one another over the muddy water holes. Some worshiped rain gods. Others sought to "witch" for water with divining rods. When the heavens turned to brass and the rains failed, crops withered and starvation spread across the land. Wells gave life.

With men toiling for days or weeks with shovels and picks, the struggle to unearth a well, with its buried treasure of life-sustaining waters, was immense—and the labor didn't cease once the well was dug. Every day included multiple trips to the well to fill countless buckets with water for the needs of the entire family; whether for cleaning, cooking, drinking or bathing, the water was all drawn from a single source.

Few people today can truly appreciate the convenience and luxury of modern indoor plumbing. Fewer still can recall teeth-chattering mornings with stiff fingers working a frozen handle on a rusty pump. Most of us, when our throats are parched, merely twist a knob, fill a glass and take a sip.

VICTORY IN THE WELLS OF ABRAHAM

Have you ever wondered what it would be like to find yourself in a wilderness with no water? Isaac, the son of Abraham, second in line of the ancient Hebrew patriarchs, experienced this very dilemma. After the death of Abraham, a famine forced Isaac to move. He transplanted his family and flocks to Gerar, a Philistine city under the control of King Abimelech.

Isaac sowed seed in that land and was blessed by the Lord with a hundredfold harvest *in the same year* (Gen. 26:12). Isaac became so wealthy, and the number of his flocks, herds and servants increased so dramatically, that his Philistine neighbors became jealous.

The Bible tells us that Abimelech kicked Isaac out of the land because Isaac was "much mightier than we" (Gen. 26:16).

Isaac was forced to pack up his entire household and move

back to the homeland of his father, Abraham. It was bad enough being evicted from his home for being too successful, but things went from bad to worse when Isaac discovered that back in his homeland his father's ancient wells had all been plugged up by the local Philistines!

The Scriptures tell us that it was envy that provoked the Philistines to these evil acts:

> And the Philistines envied him. For *all the wells* which his father's servants had digged in the days of Abraham his father, *the Philistines had stopped them, and filled them with earth.*
> —Genesis 26:14–15, emphasis added

The wells had originally been dug seventy years earlier by his father, Abraham, to supply water for his flocks, fields and family. Now all stopped up by the enemy, the wells had become useless, no longer offering access to fresh water. To reestablish himself in the parched land he had left years before, Isaac would need a boundless supply of fresh water.

Remember Them by Their Names

Upon returning to his homeland, Isaac and his servants dug out his father's wells, all of which Isaac *still remembered the names:*

> And Isaac digged again the wells of water, which they had digged in the days of Abraham his father; for the Philistines had stopped them after the death of Abraham: and he called their names after the names by which his father had called them.
> —Genesis 26:18

After Isaac had redug the ancient wells of his father, he told his men to begin digging a new well in a new location. But the herdsmen attacked Isaac's men and tried to claim the well for themselves.

> And Isaac's servants digged in the valley, and found there
> a well of springing water. And the herdsmen of Gerar did
> strive with Isaac's herdsmen, saying, The water is ours.
> —GENESIS 26:19–20

Isaac's men then dug another new well in the valley, and the locals again showed up, claiming that well as theirs, too! This is typical of the enemy, attempting to usurp what was never intended as his.

Just as Isaac did, we too will face resistance when we set out to follow God's will and obey His Word. But we must keep persevering and refuse to give up. For as you steadfastly seek to open new spiritual wells of God in your life, He will perpetually bring fresh waters of joyful rejuvenation to you.

Remember what God told Isaac as he fought the battles of the wells: "Do not be afraid, for I am with you; I will bless you…" (Gen. 26:24, NIV). Each time a battle erupted over ownership of one of Isaac's wells, he was victorious, and he would name the well after the fight that ensued. The first well was called *Strife,* and the second was called *Opposition* (Gen. 26:20–21). Just as God promised, Isaac won the battle over strife and opposition!

THE ENEMY DOESN'T WANT YOU TO HAVE THESE WELLS

Notice that until Isaac came to the valley, the herdsmen of Gerar had no interest in digging a well for themselves. They couldn't care less. It was only after someone else had come along and spent the time and effort to dig a well that they showed up and tried to claim the water as their own. Taking credit for the work of another was not unique to Isaac's time, yet he did not become discouraged when the ungodly rose up and tried to steal the prize of his labor.

The Bible says that God's people were required to walk upon the land if they wanted to possess it. God said, "Arise, walk through the land in the length of it and in the breadth of it; for I will give it unto thee" (Gen. 13:17). After they walked the land to claim it, they had to sow seed to possess it.

But it is useless to sow seed in an arid land if we don't dig a well first!

The Christian road is strewn with people who sow seed but don't bother to dig a well to irrigate and sustain the life and growth of that seed. Isaac redug old wells, dug new wells and fought for those wells as if his life depended on it—and it did! What was the result? God blessed him with victory, and the water from the wells of Isaac's father helped lay the foundation for Isaac's wealth, which empowered him to retake the land his father had long before occupied!

As you steadfastly seek to open new spiritual wells of God in your life, He will perpetually bring fresh waters of joyful rejuvenation to you.

Ours for the Taking

Some of the wells we'll visit in this book include one dug by Martin Luther, the Roman Catholic monk who, in the 1500s, boldly denounced the doctrine of salvation by works. His daring dug a well that shouted its name from the housetops, "The just shall live by *faith!*"

In England in the 1700s, John Wesley dug the well of *holiness*. I wonder how often people line up to attend a seminar on holiness. The truth of this well remains so foundational that every born-again believer needs to be on a sovereign quest to drink from the well of holiness that Wesley proclaimed over two hundred years ago.

E. M. Bounds dug the well of *prayer* during the bloody era of the American Civil War and pointed the way back to a deeper personal relationship with a heavenly Father who answers effectual, fervent prayer.

Charles Finney was moved by the Holy Spirit to renounce the religious rhetoric of his day and thereby dug a well called *revival* to call lost sinners to turn to a loving and all-powerful God.

John G. Lake brought the truth and power of a divine well of *healing* to humanity's hurting and suffering masses. Lake believed that God meant what He said in the Bible concerning health. Those who drink from that ancient well of God's healing powers have discovered that the name of Jesus and the stripes He bore possess the power to destroy pain, malady, infirmity and disease.

With God, there is an abundant supply if we return to the wells of our fathers, dig them free of the dirt of doubt and the rocks of religion and reclaim our spiritual inheritance.

Dr. Lester Sumrall obeyed God and ventured into the darkness of a demon-infested mission field to reveal to the world a holy well called *deliverance,* as he demonstrated God's power and authority over the devil and demons to an astounded church.

We owe an immense debt of gratitude to pioneers like these who showed us the way to redig the mighty wells of doctrine so that we may drink freely of their cool waters in our desert of modern humanism, pessimism, New-Ageism and worldwide anti-Christian movements.

Our society is fast becoming a spiritual Dead Sea. This sea, on the border between Israel and Jordan, is the lowest body of water on the planet—far below sea level. Although the Jordan River and several other fresh water streams pour into the Dead Sea, extreme heat causes the water to evaporate quickly, keeping the salt content lethally high. Fish that find their way into this sea do not survive. Marine life dies, except for a few plant species. Anything alive and vibrant that enters this harsh sea of death becomes stagnant and listless and dead.

The same can happen to us.

If you ever feel as if you're just barely eking out a day-to-day walk with the Lord, if your spiritual fountain is brackish and the flow of God's life-giving waters has come to a trickle, then know this: There is hope! Whatever your situation, the Lord has not forsaken you, nor will He ever. Whether your life is plagued with financial woes, sickness, depression or loved ones separated from Jesus Christ, God has already provided you with a wellspring of hope, joy, health and love—a veritable *fount of spiritual rejuvenation!*

Jesus gave a personal invitation to everyone who desires a drink of the life-giving water He alone has to give from wells He alone created.

In the Gospel of John He says, "Everyone who drinks this water will be thirsty again, but whoever drinks the water I give him will never thirst. Indeed, the water I give him will become in him a spring of water welling up to eternal life" (John 4:13–14, NIV). When you begin drinking this pure, life-giving water, it saturates you and becomes a part of your being; a spiritual *youthening* is set in motion.

Our Lord promises that this water shall be a well of living water. It will always remain in you, operating with all the freshness of eternal life. The water Jesus gives has power all its own. It is as changeless as Jacob's well, from which you can still drink today.

In our times of intense spiritual thirst, Jesus offers these words of promise:

> Whosoever drinketh of this water shall thirst again: but whosoever drinketh of the water that I shall give him shall never thirst; but the water that I shall give him shall

be in him a well of water springing up into everlasting life.

—John 14:13–14

Millions today are thirsting for truth, purity and security. With God, there is an abundant supply if we return to the wells of our fathers, dig them free of the dirt of doubt and the rocks of religion and reclaim our spiritual inheritance.

Redig Them, Drink From Them and Prosper

There are ten spiritual wells dug by our fathers who went before us—ten landmarks that the enemy has patiently worked day and night to clog up, cover over and remove from our consciousness. He uses distractions such as financial woes, health concerns, fright over rumors of war, even worry about growing old.

My prayer is that through this book, you will discover new courage to return to these important fundamental truths, these ten wells of our fathers. Perhaps you have remained faithful in digging into these wells, but have slipped in one or two areas. Maybe some of them are new to you. Whatever the case, if you will continually draw from these wells of truth, if you will let them quench your thirst for a more joyful and sustaining foundation in your life, you *will* experience God's perpetual fountain of spiritual rejuvenation and gain victorious life in Christ.

Remember all those years my Grandma Mimi would trundle up the trail, turn the crank, lower the bucket, fill it with cool, refreshing water, pull it up, fill the second bucket and then trudge back to the house, lugging two sloshing buckets with all her strength? She wore a path tromping from the house to the well and back, again and again, rain or shine, scorching heat, freezing snow, faithful as a postman. Cooking water, bathing water, cleaning water, drinking water. No mere hole in the ground, that well was a life source for Mimi, her husband, their children, Debbie and me. It was Mimi, the strongest Christian I've ever known, who discovered long ago the secret of the well: God's life-sustaining, powerful, living waters of scriptural truth.

If you will continually draw from these wells of truth, you *will* experience God's perpetual fountain of spiritual rejuvenation and gain victorious life in Christ.

Follow me and let's redig these ten ancient wells together. I fervently believe that these wells will become to you a fountain of spiritual rejuvenation that will *never* fail.

Bestseller of
All Ages

Chapter 2

Heaven and earth shall pass away, but my
words shall not pass away.
—MATTHEW 24:35

W hen the dividing wall between East and West
Berlin fell in a fury of passion for freedom several
years ago, the shock waves reverberated all the
way to Moscow. In a matter of weeks, the whole world
watched on television as angry crowds pulled down imposing
statues of Lenin from city squares. Why? Those statues sym-
bolized an era of evil in the memories of the people.

Years later, on the other side of the globe, misguided
Americans are also trying to pull down symbols, but in this
situation, they are pulling down symbols of good. Advocates
of a "religion-free" society in America have repeatedly tried
to remove God's Word from the national currency, from fed-
eral and state courtrooms, from the proceedings of legislative

bodies at every level and from our very classrooms. I am unaware of any such effort made to remove the sayings of Muhammad, Buddha or any other religious leader or fount of human wisdom from the same places.

The Bible is an amazing book, if for no other reason than because it triggers such strong reactions from people. The Bible may even draw a bigger response than any other book on the planet!

Take it upon yourself to test the way the Scriptures can change the atmosphere of a room: Lay a pocket New Testament out in full view on the table in your favorite restaurant during a busy time of day. Some of the servers there might revere that sacred Book the same way you

We are not unified by what we do *not* believe; we are joined together because of what we *do* believe.

do, and you just may receive the best service you've ever had! But others will veer around your table as if you had a live rattlesnake beside your plate!

Chances are they'll sneer at you with an expression that says, "You must be one of those fanatics who still believe in the Bible!"

Personally, I enjoy the opportunity to give them my answer: "Yes, sir! Yes, ma'am! Nothing but the Bible for me."

Such public displays of God's Word bring out strong reactions in people. I've even seen its presence separate a crowd in a public place the way the lifted rod and outstretched hand of Moses separated the Red Sea (Exod. 14:16).

A Bible boldly carried into a public place can quickly distinguish committed Christians from casual believers. True Christians will stand out from the "Sunday morning church attendees" who are openly embarrassed to be seen in public with a Bible.

Here's another experiment to try: Go to lunch at that same

18

restaurant and lay down the biggest unabridged dictionary available, and most people wouldn't give you a second glance. In many cases, they wouldn't look very hard even if someone were to lay down a copy of Hitler's *Mein Kampf.* Kahlil Gibran's *The Prophet* might get a yawn, and they might not even balk at the Quran!

Why is the Bible so important to us as Christians, and why do many people outside of the kingdom of God question its validity and relevance today? The physician Luke wrote this at the beginning of his Gospel:

> Forasmuch as many have taken in hand to set forth in order a declaration of *those things which are most surely believed among us,* even as they delivered them unto us, which from the beginning were eyewitnesses, and ministers of the word; it seemed good to me also, having had *perfect understanding of all things from the very first, to write unto thee in order*...that thou mightest *know the certainty of those things, wherein thou hast been instructed.*
>
> —LUKE 1:1–4, EMPHASIS ADDED

We are not unified by what we do *not* believe; we are joined together because of what we *do* believe. When God's Word is stolen, watered down, explained away, misrepresented or somehow withheld or isolated from believers, the church will suffer. So it was in Luther's day.

LUTHER IGNITED REFORMATION

In the year 1517, an Augustinian priest, local pastor and university theology professor named Martin Luther became so troubled by the growing abuses of "indulgence sellers" in the Catholic church (those who were trying to sell God's forgiveness) that he wrote his "95 Theses" questioning these and other abuses.

Luther declared his intention to debate publicly his points

19

and sent his complaints to a few bishops and friends. It is widely believed that Luther even nailed the letter to the door of the Castle Church in Wittenberg. Whether he did so or not, his writings became widely distributed and were so popular that three years later he wrote "An Open Letter to the Christian Nobility of the German Nation Concerning the Reform of the Christian Estate." This letter introduced three key themes that ignited reformation and earned him excommunication from Rome.

LUTHER'S FIRST THEME: *SOLA SCRIPTURA*

Sola scriptura, Latin for "Scripture only," proclaimed the Scriptures to be the only authority to which sinful man could look for a clear declaration of God's will and His plan for the redemption of mankind.

This amounted to a spiritual bombshell in Luther's day because all church services in Germany were held in Latin, a language familiar only to the priests and a highly educated few. The only Bible approved for public worship under the authority of the church based in Rome was the Latin Vulgate Bible. And it was written in Latin, a language spoken only by the educated elite! As a result, most church attendees in Germany could go to a lifetime of services without ever understanding a thing that was said, read, preached or prayed!

Church attendees today experience the same problem, except that we are without excuse. It happens every time you leave what you sense was a great meeting, yet you ask yourself in the parking lot, "What in the world were they talking about?" Or, "I haven't moved forward, I haven't been changed, and I'm still just as powerless as I ever was." Or, "I have no earthly idea what was said in that service, but at least we had a good time."

Shortly after Luther introduced his theses, he was "kidnapped" by friendly captors seeking to save his life from those who would try to kill him. He used the time in his forced seclusion to translate the Bible into German, and in just eleven months the common man had access to the holy Word of God. When the translation was completed, it was as if he had uncapped a well that was linked directly to the throne of God. Once God's Word began to reach the believers, momentum toward the Reformation became unstoppable. Perhaps this is why repressive and dictatorial governments fear the Bible in the hands of the masses!

In our own brilliant age of advanced learning and elevated intellect, highly respected theologians like Professor J. B. Pratt have proclaimed to the spiritually bankrupt and starving world that "the Bible has lost all hold on the leaders of thought and certainly is destined before many years to become one of the curiosities of the past. The inspiration of those who spake a 'thus saith the Lord' is of only a little higher type than that of the whirling dervishes and heathen medicine men."[1]

When I preach God's Word in public meetings, I often ask everyone present to take their Bibles in hand as I say: "The Book you hold in your hand contains the key to eternal life and everything that a man or woman needs from earth to heaven. Proclaim it because it is true! Men and women have died to put that Bible into your hands in a language that you can understand."

Several years ago, while in the former Union of Soviet Socialist Republics, I had the privilege of preaching the first open crusade that country had seen in seventy-five years. I still remember the moment I went to the platform and held up a Bible. I told the Russian people there, "This is a Bible. Don't ever let the atheist, the agnostic or the religious Pharisees take it from your hands. Let them take your car, let them take your home, let them take your possessions, let them throw you in jail and throw away the key. But don't ever let them take this Book from you. Make them pry it from your dead, stiff, icy fingers!"

Before I returned home from the former Soviet Union, God said, "I want you to go back to America and get on every

"Don't ever let them take this Book from you. Make them pry it from your dead, stiff, icy fingers!"

television station for which I open the door. When you get there, I want you to hold up a Bible and call America back to the basics of My Word." Needless to say, the Lord has fulfilled His word, opening prophetic doors of utterance to speak the mysteries of Christ, in accordance with Colossians 4:3.

I have been faithful to the Lord's vision. Our television program, *Breakthrough,* is now on 1,400 television stations and cable affiliates. I have been known to travel as many as 115 nights in a six-month period. I do this because I am divinely compelled to preach the truth of God's Word.

LUTHER'S SECOND THEME: *SOLA SACERDOS*

Martin Luther's second thesis, *sola sacerdos,* Latin for "sacred only," proclaimed the priesthood of all believers rather than just an elect few or some religious elite. The existing church system of that day gave the priest sole authority as man's only door to salvation, forgiveness for sins, access to the Word of God or even to be heard by the Lord in prayer.

Luther took his arguments from the Scriptures and declared anew what the Bible had long proclaimed: "Unto him that loved us, and washed us from our sins in his own blood, *and hath made us kings and priests unto God and his Father;* to him be glory and dominion for ever and ever. Amen" (Rev. 1:5–6, emphasis added).

Luther declared that no one should have to pay something (such as indulgences) to a priest to have his sins forgiven.

Jesus Christ already paid the price for our salvation—on the cross! God used Martin Luther to restore the truth that Calvary provided access to Him for all of us who come boldly to the throne of grace in our times of need and find help for our weary souls (Heb. 4:16).

LUTHER'S THIRD THEME: *SOLA FIDES*

The third thesis, *sola fides,* Latin for "faith only," simply made known and boldly declared what God Himself had stated in His Word: "The just shall live by faith" (Rom. 1:17).

You may think, *So what? Doesn't everyone know that?* But in Luther's day that statement could be considered grounds for heresy and, ultimately, a death sentence. The entire church system had been built upon a saved-by-works mentality. Once this ancient truth of salvation by faith alone was brought back into the light, this belief system began to crumble, and a mighty earthquake of freedom shook the nations.

A people in deep darkness had suddenly seen a great light. Even uneducated people in remote villages heard a rumor that Jesus Christ had already paid it all. They no longer needed a self-proclaimed mediator between them and their Savior. There was no other price to be paid, and no other man to please. They needed no one's forgiveness but God's, as stated in 1 John 2:2.

THE BIBLE IS OUR ALL-SUFFICIENT
RULE OF FAITH AND PRACTICE

What do you believe about the Bible? Is it your all-sufficient rule of faith and practice? A great general of the faith, Charles Haddon Spurgeon, once said, "This is the Bible. It is the oak of God planted in the forest of eternity entwining its roots around the Rock of Ages."

Whether you are a new Christian or a seasoned saint, you should pay close attention: The Bible is the only source of truth. It is the only rule and standard of conduct. Don't look to psychiatrists, popular magazines or even your particular denomination's creed! The Bible is the Book of Life, from Genesis to Revelation.

The Word of God is also infallible; there is *no* mistake in it! A man was reading the Bible in a park when a gentleman came up to him and asked, "Are you reading the Bible?"

"Yes, I am," the gentleman answered.

"Well," the man responded, "I wouldn't waste my time doing that. The Bible, you know, is full of contradictions."

The man reading the Bible replied, "Is that a fact?"

"Yes, sir," the gentleman said. "That's a fact. It's full of contradictions."

At that point, the man reading the Bible silently closed it, pushed it across the picnic table toward the gentleman and said, "Open it up, and show me just one." But the gentleman was at a loss to prove the man wrong.

God's Word is infallible; the Bible is inerrant. In plain terms, that means there are *no errors within its pages.* This Book has dominated the "bestseller list" for decades. No matter how many great and near-great authors, musicians, philosophers and would-be

"This is the Bible. It is the oak of God planted in the forest of eternity entwining its roots around the Rock of Ages."

saviors come along, their publications can't hold a candle to the Bible because the Bible is eternal and it is true. All of its human challengers are destined for the grave, but the Author of the Bible is the eternal, unchanging, immortal God.

THE BIBLE TELLS YOU HOW TO LIVE AND DIE

The trembling hands of people far greater than you and I have reached out and grasped hold of the Holy Bible in their dying hour. This Book not only tells you how to live, but it also tells you how to die! I like the old song that says:

Loved ones, please listen, I think you should know.
If we meet not again in this world below,
If death finds me missing and you don't understand,
There's an old Book by my bedside and it tells where I am.

—AUTHOR UNKNOWN

The authority of the Bible is a deep well in the desert of human existence. It is a source of inexhaustible refreshment, wisdom, knowledge, sustenance, strength, comfort, hope, joy, courage and purpose, which is unchanging and impervious to every circumstance and obstacle.

Every person, family, church, city, nation and society that believe and live in obedience to this Holy Book will have an abundant life, despite all odds and circumstances. Every individual and every human institution that dares to dismiss it as irrelevant, implausible or outdated will fade from view. Those who live under God's protection prosper; those who step out from under His covering wings put themselves at the mercy of a devil who knows no forgiveness.

Are you drawing from the pristine well of God's Word or from the cracked, contaminated cistern of man's wisdom and shallow philosophies? Revisit the ancient well of your fathers. Redig the well of the authority of Scriptures. Return to the Bible of your forefathers, and receive the eternal approval of your heavenly Father.

THE BIBLE CONTAINS ALL THE ANSWERS YOU'LL EVER NEED!

The answers you seek are found in the Bible. In fact, God's Word holds the keys to your basic needs and the answers to your heartfelt questions. If you need to know how to discipline your children, then get a Bible and begin reading all the Scriptures concerning children. It is a lot cheaper than therapy, and it actually works! The Bible says, "Train up a child in the way he should go: and when he is old, he will not depart from it" (Prov. 22:6). In another place it says, "Fathers, provoke not your children to wrath: but bring them up in the nurture and admonition of the Lord" (Eph. 6:4).

If you are experiencing financial difficulty, an appointment with an investment advisor should not be your first source for a solution. The greatest investor is *Jehovah Jireh,* the Lord our Provider. He gave His one and only Son, Jesus Christ, and is still reaping a harvest of souls today for the glory of His kingdom.

God's Word holds the keys to your basic needs and the answers to your heartfelt questions.

It would be better for you to invest in a Bible and sit down with God for some cutting-edge instruction in the power and ability to get wealth. Begin with Luke 6:38, "Give, and it shall be given unto you; good measure, pressed down, and shaken together, and running over, shall men give into your bosom."

Go back to the last book of the Old Testament where the prophet Malachi declared:

> Bring ye all the tithes into the storehouse, that there may be meat in mine house, and prove me now herewith, saith the LORD of hosts, if I will not open you the windows of heaven, and pour you out a blessing, that there

shall not be room enough to receive it.

—MALACHI 3:10

You can even run the devil off just by preaching the "begats" of Genesis and Matthew, if you say them with power and faith! The Bible says, "Abraham begat Isaac; and Isaac begat Jacob" (Matt. 1:2). You may be thinking, *How could talking about Abraham, Isaac and Jacob run off the devil?*

It makes the devil nervous because he knows that *Abraham was one hundred years old* when his wife Sarah gave birth to her firstborn son, Isaac. (See Genesis 21:3.) That means you are speaking words from a miracle-working Book and that the people who dare to believe it are miracle-working people!

I tell you, the Word of God holds the keys to your everyday life. From children to finances, from marriage to jobs, this Book will cause you to be successful.

THE MOST VALUABLE MANUAL FOR MARRIAGE

If you are experiencing marital strife, don't go to a marriage counselor who is promoting the latest version of the world's self-help program. Just go to a bookstore and buy a Bible! The Lord's Book is the best and most valuable marriage manual you will ever find. Consider the words of the apostle Paul:

> *Wives, submit yourselves unto your own husbands,* as unto the Lord. For the husband is the head of the wife, even as Christ is the head of the church: and he is the saviour of the body. Therefore as the church is subject unto Christ, so let the wives be to their own husbands in every thing. *Husbands, love your wives, even as Christ also loved the church, and gave himself for it;* that he might sanctify and cleanse it with the washing of water by the word, that he might present it to himself a glorious

27

church, not having spot, or wrinkle, or any such thing; but that it should be holy and without blemish. *So ought men to love their wives as their own bodies. He that loveth his wife loveth himself.* For no man ever yet hated his own flesh; but nourisheth and cherisheth it, even as the Lord the church.

—Ephesians 5:22–29, emphasis added

I have read this passage several times. But one day not long ago I read it again, and a fresh desire stirred inside of me to be a better husband. Let me say up-front that I won the heart of my wife, Joni, when we dated because I knew how to honor and respect her as a woman of God and as a lady. I'm not a casual husband, and I fully remember and appreciate why I married my wife in the first place. But on that particular day, God was working in my heart a brand-new thing on a whole new level.

Each time you pick up your Bible, you hold in your hands the answer to AIDS, to cancer, to divorce, to racism, to poverty, to sorrow and to death itself!

I prayed, "God, I want to be a better husband to Joni."

He said, *"Get in the Bible,"* so I opened my Bible and began to study.

Once again I read that I am supposed to treat Joni as Jesus would treat her. I am supposed to wait on her and I am to love her as Christ loves His church, just as we're taught in Ephesians 5:25–29. It usually doesn't take long for God to get His message across to me, and I knew this fresh emphasis from heaven called for some fresh emphasis on earth.

Joni had no idea what God was doing in me because she was out of town at the time and was scheduled to return the following evening. I called some ladies from the church and said, "Joni is gone, but she comes home tonight. I would like to hire you to help me clean the house and get the laundry done before she gets back. Would you mind coming over to help me?"

That was just the beginning, because I was on a mission from God! I went to Joni's favorite floral shop and bought her a dozen roses. Then I picked out a card I knew she would like, and I wrote a note in it telling her how much I loved her and what she meant to me. Finally, I went home and prepared dinner for her.

When Joni returned from her trip, she arrived home to a bouquet of fresh roses, a card, a clean house and a nice dinner she didn't have to prepare herself. Now, I want you to know that we had ourselves a time! Why? I made it a point to get into God's Word. I paid attention when He spoke to me about His heart for that moment, and then I did what He said. I put His Word into action. Love is a verb, my friend, and the Bible contains the answers to whatever you may need.

Each time you pick up your Bible, you hold in your hands the answer to AIDS, to cancer, to divorce, to racism, to poverty, to sorrow and to death itself!

How much of the Bible did you read this week? You may say, "Well, I just didn't have time," but if you think back, you'll realize that you had time for everything else. But is anything more important than God and His Word?

THE BIBLE IS THE CORNERSTONE UPON WHICH ALL DOCTRINE RESTS

From the time you accept Jesus Christ as your Lord and Savior until you safely arrive at your home in heaven, God's Word should be the most important thing in your life. The Bible is the cornerstone upon which all church doctrine rests. Without it, we are like ships without sails, unable to navigate through life's treacherous waters. The Bible is our moral compass, which should direct the affairs of our lives.

For too long, men have denied God's sacred Word, skirted its truths and discarded it as an outdated history book that has lost its validity in a morally bankrupt world. Even great institutions of higher learning, once renowned for their religious training, have been consumed by the new wave of liberal theology.

Former President Theodore Roosevelt once said, "A thorough knowledge of the Bible is worth more than a college education."[2] But too many of us have been faithful to feed our minds while starving our spirits. We are always learning but have yet to come to the knowledge of the truth. Then there are those among us who don't even desire to take the time to study the Bible. Being weak, they lack any real zeal to devour and digest God's Word.

The ultimate result of our negligence of the Scriptures can be found in the parable of the sower. The Word was sown four times, but the results were discouraging—only one type of soil possessed the ability to produce a harvest. Three out of four were unable to sustain the seed of the Word. (See Matthew 13:18–23; Mark 4:3–8.) No wonder the Bible has little effect in many people's lives; so often it is merely collecting dust on a bookshelf or coffee table!

The Bible should take the place of every other book, newspaper or periodical.

Once you are born again in Christ, the Bible should take the place of every other book, newspaper or periodical. Why? Because you will find eternity in its treasured pages!

The Lord placed so much importance on His Word that the psalmist declared, "For thou hast magnified thy word above all thy name" (Ps. 138:2).

ALL YOU NEED IS THE BIBLE AND THE GOD OF THE BIBLE

God's Word stands alone; this wellspring of wisdom needs no help.

You don't need any extra-biblical sources. You don't need the Bible *plus* some other religious book such as *The Book of Mormon*. You don't need the Bible and the writings of religious leaders who call upon a name other than Jesus Christ. You don't need the Bible and even the writings of the pastor of your church! The Bible and the living *God* of the Bible are *all* you need.

Why do I say you don't need anything extra to go with the Bible? Because God issued this blunt warning to John at the end of the Revelation of Jesus Christ:

> For I testify unto every man that heareth the words of the prophecy of this book, *If any man shall add unto these things,* God shall add unto him the plagues that are written in this book: And if any man shall take away from the words of the book of this prophecy, God shall take away his part out of the book of life, and out of the holy city, and from the things which are written in this book.
>
> —REVELATION 22:18–19, EMPHASIS ADDED

Why do I believe the Bible is our all-sufficient rule of faith and practice? The apostle Paul told Timothy, "All scripture is given by inspiration of God, and is profitable for doctrine, for reproof, for correction, for instruction in righteousness: that the man of God may be perfect, thoroughly furnished unto all good works" (2 Tim. 3:16–17).

The Bible is the inspired Word of God written by holy men who were inspired or "breathed upon" by God. When He breathed upon them, the words in the Bible were indelibly written in eternity as a divine edict from heaven.

WHAT DID JESUS SAY ABOUT THE SCRIPTURES?

What did Jesus say about this Book we call the Scriptures? He said, "It is the spirit that quickeneth; the flesh profiteth nothing: the words that I speak unto you, they are spirit, and they are life" (John 6:63). Matthew 24:35 tells us, "Heaven and earth shall pass away, but my words shall not pass away."

We need to fall in love with the Bible again! For those of us truly in love with the Lord, when we get up in the morning, the first thing on our minds isn't what we are going to eat for breakfast. Our first thought each day is, *Where's my Bible?* When we go to bed at night, we reach for our Bible instead of the television remote control.

One problem plaguing many Christians today is that they barely remember where their Bible is, let alone read it with interest, passion and hunger for God. They have plenty of self-help books and tapes stacked around their bed. They know the five steps to activating their faith. They rehearse the twelve steps to success, but they remain ignorant of the Word itself—God's instruction manual for His abundant life and blessings.

What we need is the Bible from A to Z. We need the Old Testament from Genesis to Malachi, and the New Testament from Matthew to Revelation.

MY PRICELESS TREASURE

Once, on a return trip home from South Africa, I put my Bible in a suitcase. To my shock, when I arrived at the airport, my suitcase hadn't arrived! I didn't care about the shoes or the suit of clothes I had inside. The cologne, the toothbrush and the sweaters I was missing all meant nothing to me. All I cared about was my Bible, the one stained with tears, personally marked with years of revelation and promises for my family and me—just another book to some, but a priceless treasure to me.

In prayer I began to ask the Lord, "In whatever time You have left for me to live in this life, if You will help me get my Bible back, I won't trust it to the hands of anyone else. For the rest of my life, I will always keep it with me!"

This went on for a week. I nearly drove everybody crazy in my grief and frustration. I went to the airport; I repeatedly called the airlines; I even called South Africa! "You just don't understand!" I told everyone who questioned my sanity. When the airlines said, "Well, we'll **The Bible holds the key to life everlasting and abundant life in this world.** give you a check to replace everything you had inside," I tried once again: "No! You don't understand. There's something in there that money can't buy—my *Bible!*"

Several days and several phone calls later I was still believing for the safe return of my Bible. My life was in that Book. It contained the Word of God plus countless numbers of notes recording divine nuggets of inspiration and revelation that God had spoken to me over the years. I didn't want to lose it.

If you have a Bible that's too holy to write in, build yourself a glass case and put it on display in a prominent place in your home so you can glance fondly at it every time you walk by. Then go out and purchase a Bible you can underline, highlight and write notes in the margin.

I have Bibles that are so marked up from years of study and meditation that you can barely recognize what the text says anymore. All you see is the revelation written all over the top of it. This was the kind of Bible that had disappeared somewhere between South Africa and Columbus, Ohio.

After nearly two weeks of lip-biting angst, I received a small tattered box from the airline. I tentatively opened it and found one pair of pants and one Bible. That's all the airline could find. Everything else was missing, but they tracked down that one pair of pants and the thing that mattered most to me—my Bible!

To ensure that nothing like that would ever happen again, I had my secretary photocopy my Bible from cover to cover. Every page of my marked-up, highlighted and footnoted Holy Book was preserved and placed in a fireproof safe. Now I have a copy of my precious Bible, no matter what might happen, safe and secure!

I love God's Word! I eat it. I drink it. I live it. I breathe it. In God's Word I have hope, and I find joy unspeakable and full of glory. Its promises range from blessing, healing, victory and dominion to wealth. The Bible holds the key to life ever-lasting and abundant life in this world. It is a refreshing well, from which I derive constant, spiritual rejuvenation.

IGNORANCE IS **NOT** BLISS

Christians must read their Bible in order to discover the wells of truth flowing from its pages. Benefiting from God's abundant supply is dependent upon our obedience to the statutes written in His Word.

The Bible declares God's view of life. His desires and promises are laid out for everyone to see. However, if you do not read *and* study your Bible, you will never know His will for you. And you will sadly discover that ignorance is not bliss.

For example, you may have heard someone say, "Well, I'm not sure if I'm going to heaven." But you will *never* find that sort of thinking in the Bible. God's Word offers a surefire cure for your doubts—simply read Mark 16:16, John 3:16–17, Acts 2:21 and Romans 10:9–10 to find out what God says about your salvation and how it came to you.

Paul sealed the question when he assured us, "For *by grace are ye saved through faith;* and that not of yourselves: *it is the gift of God: not of works,* lest any man should boast" (Eph. 2:8–9, emphasis added).

If the Bible is your all-sufficient rule of faith and practice, then you should study it as if your very life depends on it, because it does! Every thought you think must be brought under the submission of the Word. According to 2 Corinthians 10:5, every attitude of your heart must be brought under the scrutiny of this Book.

Are you one of those Christians who think the epistles are the wives of the apostles? Does it take you twenty minutes just to find the Book of Exodus? If so, you need to spend more time in your Bible! It is God's Word to *you*. Pore over it, read it, study it, cling to it—it is your unfailing guidebook through life, your perpetual fountain of truth!

THE PROOF OF DESIRE IS IN THE PURSUIT

Do you want the ability to stand upon the authority of the Word and command devils to leave in the name of Jesus? If so, are you pursuing God's Word and building up your spiritual life? Do you desire healing in your body and an abundant life here on earth? If so, how often do you crack open the Scriptures and saturate your heart and mind with its promises?

The proof of desire is in the pursuit. Many modern Christians look to everything but the Bible for answers. That leaves them in a spiritual quagmire.

The Bible alone offers the answers, guidance and comfort to any problem you will ever encounter. Unfortunately, some Christians seek "counseling" from godless authorities instead of studying *the* Authority. At our church, counseling consists of making sure the person understands the Bible concerning their situation.

Applying the principles found in the Bible is the key to solving each of life's problems. You can't blame God or your pastor for your lack of answered prayer if you choose not to heed the Word.

Examine these Scripture verses closely:

For the word of God is quick [alive], and powerful, and sharper than any twoedged sword, piercing even to the dividing asunder of soul and spirit, and of the joints and marrow, and is a discerner of the thoughts and intents of the heart.

—HEBREWS 4:12

Being born again, not of corruptible seed, but of incorruptible, by the word of God, which liveth and abideth for ever. For all flesh is as grass, and all the glory of man as the flower of grass. The grass withereth, and the flower thereof falleth away: But the word of the Lord endureth for ever. And this is the word which by the gospel is preached unto you.

—1 PETER 1:23–25

What do these verses mean to you in your own life and situation? Do you know what the Bible has to say about the problems you face? If you believe it and decree it, then you'll begin to see it, as it brings positive results into your life.

CONSUMED WITH A DESIRE

History makes it clear that you either love the Word of God or you hate it. People have tried to ban it, burn it and bury it, but God's Word has not been squelched. The truth cannot be stopped!

We must be consumed with a desire for the Word of God!

Everything comes back to Scripture. Therefore, it is important to find a church that preaches, teaches, receives and believes the Bible as God's inerrant Word!

We must be consumed with a desire for the Word of God! Job said, "Neither have I gone back from the commandment of his lips; I have esteemed the words of his mouth more than my necessary food" (Job 23:12).

We should read it in the morning, read it during our lunch hour, read it in the afternoon and read it again before we go to bed. If you don't read your Bible regularly, begin now by establishing a daily devotional time committed to its study. A good place to begin is by reading Proverbs in the morning and ending your day with the Book of Psalms.

Just as Paul commanded Timothy, "Study to show thyself approved unto God, a workman that needeth not to be ashamed, rightly dividing the word of truth" (2 Tim. 2:15), studying the Word of God will truly prepare you for the tests, trials and temptations that you will surely face in life.

THE WAY OF FREEDOM AND HOPE

The more you read and study God's Word, the more you will begin to desire it. The more of the Word you digest, the greater your appetite for it becomes. The more of His living water you drink, the thirstier you become. You will become like a man who is eating saltine crackers in the middle of the Mojave Desert. You'll be thirsty for that Book!

"And God said, Let there be light: and there was light" (Gen. 1:3). Is God's light shining in your life at this moment? Has His light permeated your mind (Rom. 12:2)? Has His light dispelled the darkness of your past? Do you understand that His Word is light and life to all of your flesh (John 1:1–4; Prov. 4:20–22)? Today, the Lord has provided His Word as "a lamp unto [your] feet, and a light unto [your] path" (Ps. 119:105).

Each time you pick up your Bible, you are holding the divine Word of God in your hands. You hold eternal truths like the truth contained in John 3:16–17:

> For God so loved the world, that he gave his only begotten Son, that whosoever believeth in him should not perish, but have everlasting life. For God sent not his Son into the world to condemn the world; but that the world through him might be saved.

In this Book are the ways of freedom and the ways of hope. In this Book are unspeakable joy and the answer to every dilemma that plagues the human mind and life.

YOU MUST BELIEVE THE BIBLE TO BELIEVE IN GOD

Is the Bible *really* that important? You can't believe in God unless you believe the Bible!

Perhaps you have noticed how confused people are about God in our society. Men, women and children are searching for God. But they seem to think they will find Him by attending a seminar given by the latest celebrated guru, reading the newest self-help bestseller or calling one of many prime-time mediums—all of which promise the "truth."

There used to be a television program called *To Tell the Truth* that had contestants choose the genuine person from among three or four people. Only one person was genuine; the others were masters of impersonation. After a round of questions from each contestant, they were asked to make their choices, and the announcer would say, "Will the *real* Rod Parsley please stand up?"

Each of the imposters would start scooting back in their chairs as if *they* were the real person. Tension would mount while everyone waited to see which person really was Rod Parsley.

That television show exemplifies the popular search for God today. The world is asking, "Will the One True God please stand up?", while it is virtually impossible for them to distinguish Him from other spiritual imposters because they have rejected His Word.

We have Muslim extremists who declare their allegiance to Allah. We have saffron-robed Buddhist monks, Hindu ascetics and New Age gurus. When all is said and done, only One will stand on that great day. He is the one Elohim, the one Jehovah. He is the one and only true and living God, and He is standing up in our hour!

How do I know that? Your Bible tells me so. It declares in eternal confidence, unequaled power and immeasurable authority:

> For I am the LORD thy God, the Holy One of Israel, thy Saviour: I gave Egypt for thy ransom, Ethiopia and Seba for thee...Ye are my witnesses, saith the LORD, and my servant whom I have chosen: that ye may know and believe me, and understand that I am he: before me there was no God formed, neither shall there be after me. I, even I, am the LORD; and beside me there is no saviour.
> —ISAIAH 43:3, 10–11

YOU NEED GO NO FURTHER

The only way to find out about the one, true God is to go to the source of all truth—the Bible. When we begin to peer into its revelations and search its truths, we need look no further than the first line of its first page where these divine words are recorded: *"In the beginning God..."* (Gen. 1:1, emphasis added).

If it is true that in the beginning there was only God, then everything that we know had to flow forth from God, the Divine Cause. Even evolutionary theory supposes that everything came from something else and that it had a new beginning. Even totally atheistic scientists acknowledge that "the beginning" sprang out of something, though they're loath to acknowledge the existence of God.

Don't be distracted, confused or thrown off course by evolutionary theories or arguments. The Bible is not the "story" of Creation. If you take that perspective, you are traveling down the wrong road. The Bible is the *facts* of Creation.

It is obvious that God was not interested in sharing with us all of the intricate details concerning the creation of the world. He could have, but He didn't. We are simply given the statement: "In the beginning God created the heaven and the earth" (Gen. 1:1). That's it. We can go forward in faith from there or stall in doubt and unbelief.

THE BIBLE IS THE DIVINE BOOK OF REDEMPTION

Your Bible presupposes that you believe what it says as Truth. If you do not believe "in the beginning God," then you will have no success believing what is said in the rest of that entire Holy Book. The Bible is not only about Creation (although I absolutely believe and preach the Creation account of the Bible); it is the divine Book of redemption!

God's emphasis from Genesis to Revelation is not on how the world was created; it is the even more mysterious process of redemption—the rebuilding, replenishing and reconstruction of the holy things of our loving God, right in the midst of the profane things of man.

The Bible is nothing less than eternity's greatest love story! Only the God of the Bible could conceive of such a thing, let alone complete it!

It is time to redig the ancient well and reestablish the landmark of the authority of the Scriptures. If the church is to go on to the next level in the purposes of God, it must return to the teachings of the Bible. Every believer

The Bible is not only about Creation; it is the divine Book of redemption!

must draw from this well where Martin Luther, a simple monk who dared to believe the Word of God, once drank of its life-giving waters.

Everything begins and ends with the inerrant authority of the Scriptures. If we read it, believe it, obey it and decree it by faith, then nothing will be impossible to us. It is time to redig this ancient well of authority and let it gush over us with life abundant.

The Cross and the Crown

Chapter **3**

God forbid that I should glory, save in the cross
of our Lord Jesus Christ.
—GALATIANS 6:14

I will never forget the first time I traveled to the land of Israel and walked the winding road that leads from Jericho to Jerusalem. As I rounded a hillside, suddenly, there laid out before me like a shimmering diamond on black velvet, was Jerusalem, city of our great King.

It was evening, and the red, blazing sun was setting in the west, casting its reflection off the stone walls of Jerusalem, turning it to gold. As I gazed down at this beautiful sight from the Mount of Olives, my eyes turned toward the Eastern Gate. Tears streamed down my cheeks as I viewed the Temple Mount where the Dome of the Rock now stands.

This mosque was built on the site of the temple. On this same mount, Abraham, in obedience to God, prepared to sacrifice his son Isaac. He slid his knife from its sheath, raised it in the air and started to plunge it into Isaac's chest when God stopped his hand in midair. In a perfect picture of what would take place centuries later on Calvary, God provided a ram for the sacrifice, and Isaac's life was spared. (See Genesis 22:1–19.)

As I continued to gaze down at the city, my eyes moved from Mount Moriah down into the Kidron Valley. I recalled that when Solomon constructed the temple on that mountain, a small stream flowed down its crevices and through the valley. When sacrifices began to be made in the temple, the crystal clear waters of that stream turned crimson red as the blood of slain sheep and goats gushed down the mountain. The brutality of the sacrifices was a reminder to the people of the seriousness of their sin and a foreshadowing of the ultimate sacrifice that was to come.

For hundreds of years, priests sacrificed animals before God for the forgiveness of sins, and the river of blood carved its way through the rock of Mount Moriah. But one Passover season, though priests still sacrificed thousands of animals and their blood still flowed into the Kidron Valley, there hung outside the city of Jerusalem a solitary figure on a lonely cross—the Lamb of God who takes away the sins of the world (Matt. 27:33–51; John 1:29, 36).

Only through the blood of Jesus Christ can mankind find peace with God and attain eternal life.

No longer would there be a need for that river of blood flowing into the Kidron Valley. No longer do we need the sacrifices of rams and goats. As I stood on the mountain that day in Israel with tears rolling down my face, I realized that the stream was once again flowing with clear water. Once and for all, our great High Priest has already entered the holy of holies, sprinkled His own blood on the mercy seat and declared, "It is finished!" (See Hebrews 9:11–15, 24–28.)

Throughout history, mankind has struggled to cope with the problem of sin and its consequences. Even cultures that do not have an understanding of Scripture and have never heard the name of Jesus possess a basic understanding of their need for redemption. There is a "sin consciousness" imbedded in the human heart that cries out to be reunited with Father God and justified in His sight.

But there is no other way for mankind to be reunited with God. Buddha did not die on a cross for his followers, and Muhammad still lies in his grave. Only through the blood of Jesus Christ can mankind find peace with God and attain eternal life.

WHO WILL PREACH THE CROSS OF CHRIST?

> For the preaching of the cross is to them that perish foolishness; but unto us which are saved it is the power of God.
>
> —1 CORINTHIANS 1:18

Much of the church today seems to have forgotten about the cross of Christ. However, we cannot effectively preach Christ without the cross. Although many might rather hear a message about the seven steps to prosperity or how to stand in faith for healing. But there can be no prosperity and there is no healing apart from what Jesus did on the cross. Even more importantly, the Bible tells us, "Without shedding of blood is no remission [of sin]" (Heb. 9:22). Having this knowledge, we have no other choice but to preach the cross and Christ crucified.

You can read the Bible from cover to cover, show up at church every time the doors are open and pray until you are blue in the face, but until you find your place at the foot of the bloodstained cross, you will not know redemption and forgiveness for your sins. For it is in Christ that we have redemption and that "through his blood, the forgiveness of sins" (Col. 1:14).

Without the cross, "religion" is futile. Without the cross, church doctrines are useless. Without the cross, communion and water baptism are nothing. Without the cross, good deeds are pointless. Without the saving, atoning work done by Jesus' broken body on Calvary, there is no way to God.

"God forbid," Paul said, "that I should glory, save in the cross of our Lord Jesus Christ" (Gal. 6:14). Salvation cannot be found in a Hindu cow, a Buddhist temple or a Shinto shrine. It's not about the church doctrines of the Baptists, the Methodists or the

We do not have to wait for God to come to us; He already has. He is waiting for us to come to Him.

Presbyterians. It doesn't matter if you speak in tongues or pray with a rosary in your hand. None of that means anything unless your beliefs are based on the old, rugged cross on which the King of glory died.

THE WAGES OF SIN IS DEATH

All you have to do to be convinced of the depravity of man is to turn on the evening news. Children are kidnapped and murdered. Stockholders are fleeced, and workers are left penniless by high-ranking executives of multimillion-dollar companies. Thousands of innocent people are killed when men full of hatred fly skyjacked planes into buildings.

Without God, we lie, cheat and steal. We murder each other in cold blood. Mankind is vile, cruel and ugly. We are hopelessly and helplessly lost without Christ. Left to our own devices, we will destroy not only ourselves, but everyone around us.

The Bible tells us that "the wages of sin is death" (Rom. 6:23). It says, "The soul that sinneth, it shall die" (Ezek.

18:4). The apostle James declares, "Sin, when it is finished, bringeth forth death" (James 1:15). The only thing we as humans truly have in common with one another is sin, and it is the one thing that no one seemingly wants to talk about.

There is only one cure for the human condition: the cross. There is no other name under heaven given among men whereby we must be saved, except the name of Jesus! (See Acts 4:12.)

"At-One-Ment" With God

The blood of Jesus Christ atones for our sins. Many Christians lack a basic understanding of what the atonement really means, but it can be explained simply by breaking the word down into three parts: at-one-ment. Christ's atonement on the cross restores our relationship, our "at-one-ment" with God. We are reconciled to God the Father through the shed blood of Jesus, and this reconciliation was preordained in ages past (1 Pet. 1:19–20). The day that the breath of life was blown into Adam's nostrils, our salvation was already determined. When Adam and Eve took of the fruit of the tree of the knowledge of good and evil, and sin first entered the human race, the cross was already in the mind of the Father. (See Genesis 3:15.) When we were yet sinners, Christ died for us (Rom. 5:8).

God provided a perfect picture in the Old Testament of what His Son would later do on the cross of Calvary. On one specific day each year, a day prescribed by God Himself, the high priest would enter the holy of holies in the temple of God to offer sacrifices for the sins of the people. This day, the holiest day in the Jewish calendar, was called the Day of Atonement (Lev. 16:29–30; 23:27–28).

Four aspects of the Day of Atonement foreshadow the saving work of Christ. When examined closely, they provide a better understanding of just what happened that day on

Calvary. We will consider each of the following aspects:

- The *person* of the atonement—the high priest who entered the holy of holies on behalf of the people

- The *procedure*—the specific actions the priest took on that day

- The *product*—the results the Day of Atonement produced

- The *perfection* of the atonement—how it has been fulfilled in the person of Jesus Christ and how it relates to our lives today

THE PERSON OF THE ATONEMENT

The Day of Atonement was a holy occasion, not to be taken lightly. Such a sacrifice was not to be made at any time by just anyone. God prescribed a certain person and a certain time for atonement to be made. Leviticus 16 declares Aaron to be the one person who could offer the sacrifice of atonement for the

One day in the pavilions of heaven, Jesus Christ laid aside His glory, His heavenly attributes, and humbled Himself to walk upon the earth in obedience to the Father's will, even to the point of death on the cross.

people. He was named the high priest, and all future priests of Israel came from his lineage. But even Aaron would suffer the penalty of death if he entered the holy of holies at the wrong time.

Just as there was a time appointed by God each year for the sacrifice of atonement to be made, there was a time appointed before the beginning of Creation in which Jesus Christ, the ultimate sacrifice, would suffer and die. (See Galatians 4:4.) Each year as the high priest entered that holy place to make atonement for the sins of the people, heaven was waiting for just that time when the blood of rams and goats would no longer be necessary. God looked forward to the day when the blood of His own Son would be shed for the remission of sins.

Let's take a closer look at this high priest. The clothing of this priestly office was, on a usual day, the most elaborate of all garments among the Israelites. The high priest wore an ephod and a breastplate made of gold. He was draped in a purple robe adorned with all manner of precious jewels, and he wore a sparkling crown upon his head. (See Exodus 28; 39.) But on the Day of Atonement, the Book of Leviticus tells us that the high priest was to lay aside all of the trappings of his office—he was to become a stripped high priest.

> He shall put on the holy linen coat, and he shall have the linen breeches upon his flesh, and shall be girded with a linen girdle, and with the linen mitre shall he be attired: these are holy garments; therefore shall he wash his flesh in water, and so put them on.
>
> —LEVITICUS 16:4

When the Day of Atonement came, the high priest stripped himself of his purple robe, his royal crown and his breastplate of gold. He laid aside all of the glory of his office and put on garments of humility.

One day in the pavilions of heaven, Jesus Christ laid aside His glory, His heavenly attributes, and humbled Himself to walk upon the earth in obedience to the Father's will, even to the point of death on the cross (Phil. 2:7–8). He became our stripped High Priest. But not only was Jesus a stripped High Priest; He was also a spotless High Priest.

It was a somber occasion when the high priest in the Old Testament entered the holy of holies. Within the chamber, incense would be burnt to cover the mercy seat where the presence of God resided. The priest had to cleanse himself thoroughly before he entered so that he would be spotless before the presence of God, and even then, the cloud of incense was a necessary shield between the holiness of God and the sinfulness of man. (See Leviticus 16.) No human being, even acting in the office of the high priest, could ever come before God completely spotless; that is, until Jesus Christ walked the earth. Jesus became our spotless High Priest and took upon Himself the sins of the world.

For this reason, the virgin birth is so important to our Christian faith. Some preachers today would like to say that Jesus was not truly born of a virgin, but to say such a thing is to deny the divinity of Christ. And, friends, if Christ is not divine, if He does not have the sinless blood of His Father flowing through His veins, He could not have been a spotless sacrifice—and our very salvation is in jeopardy. Only a sinless One could take our place, the place of a sinner. Thank God that the virgin birth was real and that the incarnation of Christ, the God-man, brought forth our spotless High Priest. (See Matthew 1:23.)

Not only was Jesus a stripped, spotless High Priest, He was solitary as well. On every other day of the year, the priests in the temple would help one another prepare the sacrifices in the morning and the evening. But on the Day of Atonement, the high priest was to have no assistance; he was to make all preparations himself. (See Leviticus 16:5–28.)

It is very interesting to note that for three years Jesus had a band of followers with Him almost at all times. They listened to His teachings, watched Him heal the sick and saw Him raise the dead. They even declared their undying love for Him. When the time came, they were unable to stay awake to pray with Him as He poured His heart before His Father in Gethsemane. And when He was arrested by a band of soldiers, they scattered like lost sheep without a shepherd (Matt. 26:36–58).

Jesus died alone, hung between two thieves like a common criminal (Matt. 27:38). The Lord of glory, who could have called ten thousand angels to His aid with a movement of His finger, chose to die alone, a solitary High Priest atoning for the sins of the world.

Finally, on the Day of Atonement, the high priest is a strenuous high priest. Without help from any other person, he had to slaughter fifteen animals in that single day. He would plunge the knife into the heart of the goat and literally tear its body apart. The blood of the sacrifices would drip down his arms, off of his elbows, onto his garments, until it covered his entire body (Lev. 16:4). He was laboring strenuously before God for the sins of the people.

Can you see Christ, our Lord, in Gethsemane? Can you see Him as He prays, the sweat pouring off His body in drops of blood (Luke 22:44)? Can you sense the weight of your sin on His shoulders—the press of your transgressions, your lies, your immorality, your cheating, stealing and conniving, all of your sin?

Can you see Him in Pilate's hall as the Roman soldiers rip His back open with a cat-o'-nine-tails? Its leather thongs contain bits of glass and bone in the ends so that they might better tear His flesh from His body until the bones of His ribs are exposed. Can you see Him as they press the crown of thorns into His head and blood pours down His face?

He is kicked. He is beaten. He bears the heavy weight of a wooden cross throughout the streets of Jerusalem. He carries the sins of the entire world upon His shoulders. Yes, ours is a strenuous High Priest.

THE PROCEDURE OF THE ATONEMENT

The procedures to be followed on the Day of Atonement were unlike those followed on any other day of the year.

On the Day of Atonement, two goats were brought to the

high priest for use in the ceremony. Both hold great significance to the picture of what Christ did for us on the cross. As the two goats stood before him, Aaron drew lots to determine which would be used as a sacrifice and which would become the scapegoat (Lev. 16:8).

The unlucky goat, the one to be used for the sacrifice, was chosen by God through lots to be the first sacrifice of the new year. Watch as its blood is spilt, as Aaron slits its throat and its eyes roll back in its head in death. Its blood runs through Aaron's hands and onto the altar of the Lord in a foreshadowing of the ultimate sacrifice to come (Lev. 16:8–9, 15–16).

See the Lord Himself, marred beyond recognition, carrying the weight of the cross through the streets of Jerusalem. As Golgotha is reached, He is stretched out on the beam and nails are driven through His hands and feet. He is lifted high upon the cross. The blood flows down, the sacrificial blood shed for you and me (John 19:16–18).

What happens to the second goat, the one chosen as the scapegoat for the people? Surprisingly, it is allowed to live. Aaron places his blood-soaked hands on the head of that goat and speaks aloud the sins of the people; the sins of the entire nation of Israel are put on the head of that goat, and then it is led away (Lev. 16:21–22).

The goat is led outside the city for one day, then two; it is led away for a duration of ten days. Then the one who has led the goat into the wilderness releases it and watches it run away, disappearing from view into the horizon. He then returns to the priest and shares the news, "Our sin, on the bloody head of that goat, is gone! It is far removed from us, and we will never see it again."

This living goat is a symbol of our living, risen Savior. Jesus Christ was first a sacrifice, but then He conquered death and the grave. There was one goat that could not be killed—the goat that has removed our sins from us as far as the east is from the west (Ps. 103:12).

If you were to travel north, you would eventually reach the North Pole. Once you had passed it, you would be traveling south. In other words, you can't travel north forever. If you begin by traveling due east, no matter how far you travel, you will never reach the west. That's how far Jesus has removed our sins from us—we could travel forever and still not reach them!

THE PRODUCT OF THE ATONEMENT

What was the result of the Day of Atonement? In ancient Israel, the forgiveness of sins was attained for yet another year. The high priest was allowed to enter the presence of God, beyond the veil, on that one holiest of holy days of the year. **The greatest product of the atonement is the *at-one-ment* with God.** Aaron would walk through the outer court, where most of the people waited, and through the inner court, which was lit by the golden lampstand. He would pass through the veil into the holy place, where the smoke of the incense created a barrier between God and him, lest he should stand directly in God's presence and die.

On one particular Passover, as the Lamb of God hung on the cross and died, the veil in the temple—the veil that was four inches thick, forty feet wide and twenty feet high—was torn in two from top to bottom (Matt. 27:15). As Jesus uttered the words, "It is finished," the final sacrifice had been made (John 19:30). God was in effect saying to mankind, "Come on in, My beloved children. Come into My presence and worship Me face to face!"

As I have said before, the greatest product of the atonement is the *at-one-ment* with God that it purchased for every man, woman, boy and girl who would choose to bathe themselves in the precious blood of Jesus and enter the holy of holies to stand in the presence of God.

THE PERFECTION OF THE ATONEMENT

We have seen the person, the procedure and the product of the atonement, but what is its perfection? How do we see its completion, especially in our own lives?

When the Day of Atonement was instituted in the Old Testament, the high priest was not the only one who was given instructions to follow. The children of Israel were commanded to prepare their hearts for that day by "afflicting their souls." (See Leviticus 23:27.) Now, I am all for praise and worship services in which we clap our hands and dance before the Lord, but there is a time and a place to afflict our souls, to reflect on the great price that was paid for our redemption. The great hymnist Isaac Watts said it like this:

> *When I survey the wondrous cross*
> *On which the Prince of glory died,*
> *My richest gain I count but loss,*
> *And pour contempt on all my pride.*[1]

When you think of who you are, who He is and what He became for you, does it afflict your soul? Can you do nothing but bow your face before Him and cry out, "I am the sinner, and You, Lord, are the Savior"?

The second thing the children of Israel were to do was cease from all work on that day. Paul declared that this salvation is "not of works, lest any man should boast," but "by grace are ye saved through faith" (Eph. 2:8–9). You don't have to work for your salvation. You don't have to struggle to please God. All you must do is cease from your labors, afflict your soul and bow before the old, rugged cross.

At the end of that day, the final perfection took place. The high priest, after he had slain fifteen animals and completed all of the ceremonies, would return to his dressing chamber, remove his bloodied garments and wash his body from head to toe. Then he would walk to where he had left his purple robe and put it back on his shoulders. He would place the golden breastplate on his chest and set the royal crown back on his head. The high priest, once again adorned in his bejeweled garments of authority, would walk back out to the congregation of Israel and declare, "The work has been completed." (See Leviticus 16:23–24, 32–33.)

We serve a risen Savior! He has conquered death, hell and the grave, and He has taken back upon Himself His royal garments of authority! Today He is seated at the right hand of the Father, and when you bring your sin before Him, He points to the mercy seat and shows the Father His own shed blood (Rom. 8:34; Heb. 10:12).

The work has been completed. Your salvation has been paid for. All you need do is accept the free gift Jesus offers you with outstretched hands (Eph. 2:8–9). If you have never prayed the prayer of salvation before or if you wish to renew your commitment to your risen Savior, I ask you to join with me in the following prayer:

> *Heavenly Father,*
>
> *I come before You today as a sinner, knowing I have disobeyed Your laws and deserve Your judgment. I confess these sins to You now, and I ask You to forgive me of my sins.*
>
> *Lord Jesus, wash me in Your blood. I come to You as the great High Priest, and today becomes my day of atonement. Thank You, Lord Jesus, for Your sacrifice for me! Fill my life with Your presence. Let me know Your forgiveness, and give me the assurance that I am on my way to heaven.*
>
> *In Jesus' name I pray, amen.*

There is no greater well to redig than the precious well of the atonement for sins. Continue to revisit this well again and again in your life, and drink deeply of its living waters.

This Holy Well

Chapter 4

*But as he which hath called you is holy, so be ye
holy in all manner of conversation; because it is
written, Be ye holy; for I am holy.*
—1 PETER 1:15–16

I magine a world so devoid of God and His truth that anyone who dared take a stand for Him puts his or her very
life in jeopardy. The idea of a personal God and a moral-
ity based on eternal values of right and wrong are mocked.

Universities once founded to train devout young men for
the ministry are so overrun by liberal theologians and agnostic professors that the remaining few who actually still believe
in the Scriptures run for cover to avoid ridicule and abuse
from their classmates.

The media take grand potshots at anyone foolish enough
to preach from the Bible. Church members under these pastors' leadership hate them so much that they torch their
homes, kill their pets and livestock, threaten their children

openly from the street and send an armed mob regularly to "serenade" the pastor's family with ungodly, loud noises until past midnight week after week.

The most "successful" churches of the day thrive on flowery sermons designed to appeal to intellectualism, removing any hint of emotion or passion from the service. Anyone who preaches outside of this standard is publicly scorned.

Are we headed there—or have we already been there?

This is the world into which Samuel and Susanna Wesley's fifteenth of nineteen children was born. Young John barely escaped death in a fire purportedly started by his pastor-father's "congregants" who hoped to run him off because he preached the truth. Only a miracle of God saved John after he was trapped on the second floor of a house engulfed in flames.[1]

THEY REFUSED TO ABANDON
THEIR HATEFUL FLOCK

Despite false imprisonment, the burning of his meager crops and continual threats of physical harm and death, Samuel and Susanna Wesley stood the test and refused to abandon their hateful flock or to grow bitter over the people's obstinacy:

> He had come to Epworth poor; now, fifteen years later, he was poorer, having doggedly served his parishioners only to have them detest him.
>
> But, he stood unbeaten; and as he stared out his window there gripped him—not for the first time, a fierce ironical affection for the hard landscape, the fields of his striving, even the folk who had proved such good haters …With him as with many, true men disappointed in his fate, his hopes passed from himself to fasten the more eagerly on his sons. He wanted them to be great and eminent soldiers of Christ, and he divined already that if for one above the others, this eminence was reserved for John.[2]

John Wesley's father was right—God had anointed his son to redig the ancient well of holiness unto the Lord, and he would do it in the midst of one of the most profane and volatile periods in Western history.

John had been taught well by the perseverance of his righteous father. He studied and became a minister of the Church of England, but he discovered that, in and of himself, he wasn't enough for the task at hand. He still lacked something that would make all the difference. This lack became obvious when the young clergyman made a transatlantic voyage to the American colonies to preach among the Indians and completely failed in the attempt.

"I WENT TO CONVERT THE HEATHEN—BUT WHO WILL CONVERT MY OWN SOUL?"

On Wesley's return trip to England nearly two and a half years later, two things happened. First, he committed to paper the growing conviction in his heart: "I went to America to convert the heathen. But who will convert my own soul?"[3] Wesley went on to say: "I have a fair summer religion, I can talk well…and believe myself while no danger is near. But let death stare me in the face and my spirit is troubled, nor can I say to die is gain."[4]

The second life-changing incident in Wesley's journey occurred when the ship returning them to England was nearly inundated with a great wave in a fierce Atlantic storm. The force of the wave split the mainsail and showered the deck with debris.

While all of the English passengers cursed or cried out for their lives in fear, Wesley noticed that the German Moravians aboard remained absolutely calm in the face of death—even the women and children. A Moravian leader named Peter Bohler calmly led his flock in hymns while the rest of the passengers and crew battled paralyzing fear.

Wesley asked one of the Moravian men if he was afraid during the crisis. He answered, "Thank God, no." When Wesley further asked about the women and children, the man matter-of-factly said, "Our women and children are not afraid to die."[5]

This peace in the face of grave peril and certain death intrigued Wesley—so much so that upon his return to London, he searched out the Moravians to determine what made them so different from other people.

WESLEY'S HEART WAS "STRANGELY WARMED"

The English clergyman began to attend Moravian meetings in London, and so began his three-month search for the truth. Finally, one night during a Moravian watch night prayer service on Aldersgate Street in London, Wesley's life was transformed. It was there that he felt his heart "strangely warmed" by the fire of the Holy Spirit.[6] In that moment, Wesley went beyond the theology of the cross to finally meet the risen Savior of that cross.

He caught an ember from the fiery Moravian believers who knew the task and smell of victory in the face of persecution, and a fresh fire was stirred in his bonds. John Wesley then began to drink deeply of the anointing

Oh, for righteous men and women who will dare to live lives of sacrificial service above and beyond reproach!

found only in the deep waters of the well of holiness unto God. He had been set apart for a holy mission.

In the meantime, Samuel Wesley had died and was buried in Epworth. When John Wesley returned to claim his father's pulpit, the curate of Epworth, who had been standing in until Wesley's arrival, refused to let Wesley enter his father's church.

Denied the right to preach in his father's church, Wesley

took his stand on the one piece of family property that no one could take from him—his father's grave! He stood on his father's tombstone in the church cemetery and preached the unpopular truths of justification by faith to all who would come night after night! For eight nights Wesley preached with passion in the graveyard.

> [Romely, the curate of Epworth] had miscalculated Wesley's flock; this stubborn English breed so loyal in enmity, loving the memory of a foe [Samuel Wesley] who had proven himself a man.[7]

Oh, for more men like John Wesley, who will prove themselves genuine men of God in the midst of opposition, rejection and persecution. Oh, for more brave women like Susanna Wesley, who proved herself more than a match for every evil attack of the enemy and who raised her children to do the same! Oh, for righteous men and women who will dare to live lives of sacrificial service above and beyond reproach!

NOTHING LESS THAN HOLINESS WILL STAND THE TEST

My friend, whether you are a preacher, a teacher, a layman or a new disciple of Jesus Christ, drink deeply and fully from the well redug by John Wesley—the well of holiness, sanctification and godly separation unto God! Nothing less will stand the test. No less than such a purity possesses the power to properly carry God's gospel to the lost and dying world.

There is only one cure for compromise, sin and double-mindedness—holiness unto a holy God. John Wesley tirelessly preached the doctrines of holiness, purity and separation unto God for sixty-five years until he died at the age of eighty-eight.

A TALL ORDER

Wesley required every candidate for the Methodist ministry to live holy, serve humbly, work tirelessly, study God's Word diligently and pray without ceasing. That is a tall order for today's vocational preacher!

According to author and revival researcher Winkie Pratney, John Wesley "left behind him 750 preachers in England and 350 in America; 76,968 Methodists in England and 57,621 in America."[8] He obviously practiced what he preached.

Wesley rose every day at 4:00 A.M. and traveled 225,000 miles over the next fifty-two years (mostly by horse) and preached more than fifty thousand sermons! He traveled an average of twenty-five miles per day yet managed to write 233 books on a wide variety of subjects (even electricity). He also published fifty volumes of theology, wrote a commentary on the entire Bible and carefully directed and guided the ministries of Methodist pastors.[9]

The typical candidate for ministry in America faced the constant threat of death on the frontier from disease, Native American Indians (who controlled much of the middle and western regions), hostile audiences and the constant dangers of travel. Methodist ministers in England fared little better.

Elmer Towns and Douglas Porter said in *The Ten Greatest Revivals Ever*:

> The typical Methodist itinerant preacher...traveled 200 to 500 miles in a monthly circuit on horseback, had 30 to 50 preaching locations plus classes—and received only $64 a year. The circuit riders slept in homes, at inns or in the open field.
>
> ...They never read their sermons, as the Anglicans or Congregationalists did, but instead exhorted the people passionately from the Bible, using anecdotes, illustrations, and analogies from everyday life. They learned how to preach passionately by listening to passionate

preaching. *Yet it was not their oratory that won their audiences. It was their power.*

...By the end of the Revolutionary War, only sixty Methodist chapels had been built, but the circuit-riding preachers used cabins, inns, schools—any place to preach the gospel. With time, each preaching point built a chapel, giving stability and influence to the Methodist movement. By the mid-1800s, it had become the largest Protestant denomination.[10]

ARE YOU IN YOUR RIGHT MIND?

No one in their right mind would have chosen to be a Methodist minister under those conditions. (Some believed that living as a Methodist convert was almost as tough!) Methodist circuit riders received virtually no salary, had no church building or pulpit to call their own, lived out of their saddle-bags, depended on the grace of God and the hospitality of the people they met and were often scorned and rejected—especially by those in established Christian churches.

When sin-sick people see believers walking in holiness and purity—and offering a way out of the filth and bondage of sin—they will want to know more.

The Methodist ministry was a *faith* ministry demanding the highest standards of holiness and a burning passion for the lost. Oh, to see the old Methodist fire sweep through this nation—and the ranks of the ministry—once again!

These humble ministers of the gospel were required to fast at least one day per week for their entire lives, and John Wesley constantly demanded that they read the Scriptures, avoid alcohol and rise early every morning. He knew that personal discipline and holiness before the Lord go hand in hand. (How many seminaries today are teaching this foundation of holiness in ministry?)

The Methodist movement, launched as part of the First Great Awakening, is credited by many for saving England from the violence that nearly destroyed France in the French Revolution. It also powerfully influenced the new American nation.

Wesley's devotion to God and a holy life strongly influenced George Whitefield, Charles Finney and Walter and Phoebe Palmer, whose work in America dominated American revivalism for thirty years and helped launch the revival of 1857–58.[11]

In our own day, too many are confused, believing that God's blessings are an indication of our holiness. To that end, many won't go into the ministry unless they are assured of a good living, as little risk as possible and attractive surroundings.

Don't even talk about daily prayer, diligent Bible study ("Been there, done that in Bible college"), fasting ("You mean people still believe in that?") or a servant's heart ("I'm better than that job—I paid dearly for my degree!").

NO COMPROMISE

When John Wesley stood up on his father's tombstone to pick up the standard of holiness that his parents had lived out, he raised it even higher through the power of the Holy Spirit! It's time to redig that well of holiness and raise the standard once again. It is time to restore the time-proven biblical standards of moral integrity, physical purity and spiritual intensity.

Christians don't have to stand idly by and be content with a standard of holiness that imitates the world's decadent music with copycat Christian music. Nor do we have to buy into the current standard that asserts, "Well, you see, Pastor, we gotta be like 'em in order to win 'em. Everybody knows that."

Is that so? Jesus didn't think so. John Wesley didn't think

so, and I don't think so. Everybody loses when Christians compromise.

You and I have only one thing to offer the world that they can't get anywhere else in creation—the unchanging gospel of Jesus Christ. This message is not some watered-down, secondhand, whitewashed package draped with the trappings of dead religion. Again, compromise won't cause the world to turn to the Savior. But when sin-sick people see believers walking in holiness and purity—and offering a way out of the filth and bondage of sin—they will want to know more.

"MOTHER, WHAT IS SIN?"

When we redig the well of holiness and raise its standard, our example will lead others to do the same. John Wesley's mother had a great deal to do with his success in the ministry. It has been said that as a teenager, John went to his mother and asked, "Mother, what is sin?"

She answered him, "John, sin is anything that impedes the tenderness of your conscience."

She also told him, "It is anything that obscures your sense of God." That would include anything that weakens your reason or dulls your desire for spiritual things.

Don't be fooled by all of the slick words people throw around. To permit a thing is the same thing as to participate in that thing. Too many of us assure our friends and spiritual leaders, "I would never do that." Yet, for some odd reason, we think nothing of spending $8.00 to go into a darkened movie theater and watch somebody else do it and enjoy it.

God's final word on holiness: *It is not an option.*

Winkie Pratney drew a powerful conclusion to his book *Revival: Principles to Change the World* that echoes some of the statements I've made about paying the price for holiness before the Lord and true power in our ministry among the lost:

> When the question is asked: "What hinders revival?" one of the simple answers is this: We do not have men and women who are prepared to pay the same price to preach the same message and have the same power as those revivalists of the past. Without these firm believers, the community can never be changed. Our concern is conciliatory, our obedience optional, our lack theologically and culturally justified. Quite simply, it costs too much!
>
> We say we want revival. But who today is prepared to live a life of absolute obedience to the Holy Spirit, tackling sin in the Church as well as the streets, preaching such a message of perfection of heart and holiness of life—a message feared and hated by the religious and the street sinner alike? Are we prepared?[12]

HOLINESS IS NOT AN OPTION

We will end as we began with God's final word on holiness: *It is not an option.* Peter declares these words:

> But as he which hath called you is holy, so be ye holy in all manner of conversation; because it is written, Be ye holy; for I am holy.
>
> —1 PETER 1:15–16

Sweet Hour
of Prayer

Chapter 5

Men ought always to pray, and not to faint.
—LUKE 18:1

All of the great leaders of the Bible drank at the oldest well of our fathers—the ancient well of effectual and fervent prayer. Abraham prayed that God would spare the wicked cities from His wrath. (See Genesis 18.) David spent time in prayer both before and after he became king of Israel. (See 1 Samuel 30:8; 2 Samuel 7:18–29.) The prophet Daniel made prayer such a daily discipline that his enemies were able to predict the time each day when he would be on his knees. (See Daniel 6:10–11.)

Even the King of glory, Jesus Himself, drank continually from the well of prayer. One night in the Garden of Gethsemane, under the light of a Passover moon, Jesus agonized in His Father's presence, spending hours in prayer concerning the cross He was about to face. Even after an angel strengthened Him, He went to prayer again, and even more fervently communed with the Father—to the point that His sweat became like great drops of blood. (See Luke 22:42–44.)

When was the last time you faced a need so traumatic, so desperate that you found yourself falling to your knees? Do you look forward to pouring your heart out to your Father each day in prayer? Do you crave the time spent in His sweet presence, basking in His love and soaking in His goodness?

Prayer has been the backbone of godly revelation, action and power since the beginning of time.

Most of us rush through our prayer time—that is, if we even have a bona fide prayer time at all. By doing so, we fail to realize that we are missing out on the most important aspects of our faith: one-on-one communication with the God of the universe and the strengthening of our relationship with the Lover of our souls.

Prayer has been the backbone of godly revelation, action and power since the beginning of time. It will continue to be the foundation even when time is no more and we are ushered into God's presence to spend eternity there. In the Book of Revelation, the heavenly prayers of the saints become fragrant offerings that move the heart of God and signal cataclysmic changes in heaven and on earth:

> And when he had taken the book, the four beasts and four and twenty elders fell down before the Lamb, having every one of them harps, and golden vials full of odours, which are *the prayers of saints*...And another angel came and stood at the altar, having a golden censer; and there was given unto him much incense, that he should offer it with the prayers of all saints upon the

golden altar which was before the throne. And the smoke of the incense, which came with the prayers of the saints, ascended up before God out of the angel's hand.
—REVELATION 5:8, 8:3–4, EMPHASIS ADDED

"WITHOUT PRAYER, THE CHURCH IS LIFELESS"

In our nation's darkest hours, during a bloody Civil War that pitted brother against brother and father against son, God raised up a man named E. M. Bounds to proclaim anew the necessity of prayer. Very few people listened to him during his lifetime, but his legacy speaks louder than ever today.

E. M. Bounds devoted forty-six years of his life to the ministry of prayer. He wrote eight classic books on prayer—yet he was virtually unknown at the time of his death, and only two of his books were published during his life. This anointed man was not sent forth to become famous; he was sent to comfort the afflicted and to afflict the comfortable with his burning message on prayer.

He spent three to four hours a day in impassioned prayer and expected everyone else to do the same if they claimed to be ministers of the gospel. He often made other ministers uncomfortable with his call to holiness and his sanctified life of disciplined prayer. His prayer-soaked writings brought the conviction of the Holy Spirit to churches and preachers alike:

> The life, power and glory of the church is prayer. The life of its members is dependent on prayer. The presence of God is secured and retained by prayer. The very place is made sacred by its ministry. Without it, the church is lifeless and powerless. Without it, even the building itself is nothing more than any other structure. Prayer converts even the bricks, mortar and lumber into a sanctuary, a holy of holies, where the Shekinah dwells.[1]

EVEN JESUS HAD TO PRAY!

Jesus modeled a lifestyle of prayer for us, as shown in the

God longs for us to rediscover the power of that old-fashioned "sweet hour of prayer."

Gospels. Have you noticed in your study of the Bible that *even Jesus had to ask His Father for the things He needed on earth?* Even though He was Lord and possessed all dominion and authority, while on earth He had

to operate according to the laws set forth by God for all humans. (See Genesis 1:26–27; John 10:1–2.)

God Himself declared in the Book of Psalms: "Ask of me, and I shall give thee the heathen for thine inheritance, and the uttermost parts of the earth for thy possession" (Ps. 2:8). God said of His people Israel: "It is my will to do it, but *I will be inquired of* by them concerning it first." (See Ezekiel 36:37.)

It is true; even Jesus had to pray: "And I will pray the Father, and he shall give you another Comforter, that he may abide with you for ever" (John 14:16). If He had to approach His Father in prayer, then surely we can understand His instruction to us:

> So I say to you, *ask,* and it will be given to you; *seek,* and you will find; *knock,* and it will be opened to you. For everyone who asks *receives,* and he who seeks *finds,* and to him who knocks *it will be opened.*
> —LUKE 11:9–10, NKJV, EMPHASIS ADDED

A GOD WHO ANSWERS PRAYER

Jesus' instruction in Luke 11 not only reminds us of our need to spend time with the Father in prayer, but it also tells us of the Father's response when we do. He will listen! He will open the door! He will provide!

Remember the words of James: "Ye have not, because ye ask not" (James 4:2). I don't know who came up with the idea that God doesn't answer prayer. All I see in the Scriptures is the God whom Jesus described in the Gospel of Mark:

> Have faith in God. For verily I say unto you, That whosoever shall say unto this mountain, Be thou removed, and be thou cast into the sea; and shall not doubt in his heart, but shall believe that those things which he saith shall come to pass; he shall have whatsoever he saith. Therefore I say unto you, What things soever ye desire, when ye pray, believe that ye receive them, and ye shall have them.
>
> —MARK 11:22–24

God longs for us to rediscover the power of that old-fashioned "sweet hour of prayer." A brief prayer mumbled somewhere between the on-ramp of the freeway and the fast-food window where we grab an egg muffin and coffee on the way to work is not enough! That is not characteristic of a prayer life based on a vibrant relationship with a living God—it is the fulfillment of an obligation, and a half-hearted fulfillment at that. Such "prayer" can never fill the longing of either the Father's heart or your own.

"COULD YE NOT WATCH WITH ME ONE HOUR?"

Jesus still calls out to believers just as He called to the slumbering disciples in the Garden of Gethsemane: "What, could ye not watch with me one hour?" (Matt. 26:40).

Once again I hear the passionate voice of E. M. Bounds rising from the well as he digs with all of his strength to clear the way for fresh water to flow in this area of our lives. He calls to the sleepy church:

> True prayer must be aflame. Christian life and character

75

need to be on fire. Lack of spiritual heat creates more infidelity than lack of faith. Not to be consumingly interested about the things of heaven is not to be interested in them at all. The fiery souls are those who conquer in the day of battle, from whom the kingdom of heaven suffers violence, and who take it by force. The citadel of God is taken only by those who storm it in dreadful earnestness, who besiege it with fiery, unabated zeal.

Nothing short of being red-hot for God can keep the glow of heaven in our hearts these chilly days.[2]

I hear another voice, the voice of Andrew Murray. Hear him as he too calls us to drink from the well of fervent prayer:

[This] is the secret of the life of prayer. Take time in the inner chamber to bow down and worship; and wait on Him till He unveils Himself, and takes possession of you, and goes out with you to show how a man may live and walk in abiding fellowship with an unseen Lord.[3]

PAY THE PRICE; SEEK HIS FACE; SURRENDER ALL TO HIM

Why do we believe we can live the victorious Christian life without prayer when even the Son of God needed times of fervent prayer just to go from day to day? No preacher is fit to speak to God's people until he has first paid the price in prayer to hear the heart of the Father concerning His people. No Christian can claim to be fully equipped and prepared to live for Christ until he or she first pays the price to seek His face and surrender all to Him.

Once, during a major series of meetings, I called the congregation to the front of the building and said, "There's an urgency here tonight. Pray!"

Those precious people just stared at me. They tried to pray. With the best of intentions they fumbled around without a clue. My heart was pierced with a thousand sorrows. I hung my head and began to weep.

Where are the mothers who will teach us to pray? Where are the prayer warriors who show up early at meetings—not to get the best seat, but to pray for an hour before the service begins?

I grew up in a Baptist church that didn't believe in a modern Pentecost experience, but the mothers still showed up an hour before the service to walk back and forth across the front of the church praying, "God, crown these altars with souls! Give us souls lest we die! Give us victory at this altar tonight!"

> **No Christian can claim to be fully equipped and prepared to live for Christ until he or she first pays the price to seek His face and surrender all to Him.**

You say, "I can't do anything with my teenager." Have you brought him or her to the Lord in prayer?

You may be saying, "My marriage is falling apart." How much time have you spent in prayer about the situation?

I have been told a story about the late John Osteen that bears repeating. He was walking through his home one day when his wife, Dodie, suddenly jumped up on his back, wrapped her arms around him and locked her legs around his waist. They had been in an argument, and she told him, "I'm not letting you go until we pray. I refuse to let you go until we pray." (See Ephesians 4:26.) Now that is how you maintain a marriage!

TEACH US TO PRAY

My daughter comes into my bedroom every Saturday night and says, "Daddy, I'm ready to go to bed now." I know what she really means—"It's time to pray!" She is about to lay those little thirteen-year-old hands on Daddy and pray for the Holy Spirit to move in his life.

I still remember the time I was pulling out of the driveway

The secret to power in the midst of the stress of your everyday life is to learn to pray and not faint.

when my little boy came over and had me stop the car. He opened the door and said, "Come here, Daddy. Let me pray for you." Then he laid his hands on me and started to pray—right there in the driveway!

O Lord, give us a praying church, not a playing church. Give us a ministering church! Reignite fires of prayer in our hearts!

We have too many preachers spending more time in marketing meetings than they do in the prayer closet. We need more "schools of prayer" like the one Smith Wigglesworth—that great general of the faith—had for a young preacher named Lester Sumrall.

It was a foggy day when Smith Wigglesworth heard someone knock at his door. "Good morning, sir," the visitor said. "I'm Lester Sumrall."

"What's that under your arm, Sumrall?"

"Why, it's a newspaper, sir."

"You'll have to leave that outside. We read nothing in this house but the Bible. Come with me, lad."

Into his chambers they went. "This is my pattern," said Wigglesworth. "We shall now read the Word together for thirty minutes."

When the time had elapsed, he said, "Thirty minutes are now up. We shall now close our Bibles, and we shall prostrate ourselves before the throne of grace. We shall call upon the might and dominion of God's power that He might perchance by grace and mercy reveal to us some truth for hurting humanity. Let us pray."

And so for thirty minutes they prayed. Lester Sumrall then watched Smith Wigglesworth rise from his kneeling position and settle back into his seat, where he opened the Bible again and read for another thirty minutes.

After that time, they prayed for another thirty minutes, and then read the Word for another half-hour shift. There was no TV, no HBO, no movies, no popcorn. When the clock struck 11:30 A.M., Smith Wigglesworth announced it was time for lunch. Thirty minutes later the meal was finished, and Mr. Wigglesworth said, "Come back to the chambers, Sumrall."

You guessed it. Once again they read God's Word for thirty minutes and prayed for thirty minutes. This continued throughout the afternoon, and again the next day, and the following days of the "prayer school."[4]

If you ever wonder why we can't perform the miracles that they did, it is because we don't practice the disciplines they did! If we ever hope to live in victory and minister in power, we must learn to travail and wait upon God in prayer. The secret to power in the midst of the stress of your everyday life is to learn to pray and not faint.

SEVEN MAJOR TYPES OF PRAYER

The Lord makes it clear in His Word that prayer is vital to His purposes both for the church and for our lives. He wants us to learn how to flow smoothly between the seven major types of prayer as He leads us in our journey of faith. This keeps us from losing heart and giving up just before He comes through on our behalf.

1. Pray the prayer of authority.

Jesus said in Matthew 16:19, "And I will give unto thee the keys of the kingdom of heaven: and whatsoever thou shalt bind on earth shall be bound in heaven: and whatsoever thou shalt loose on earth shall be loosed in heaven."

How do you pray the prayer of authority? You learn how

to "bind and loose" in the name of Jesus:

> *Lord Jesus Christ, I confess this day that I speak the law of the Lord. I am Your child because You have begotten me. I am anointed. You have anointed me to preach the gospel to the poor and to heal the broken-hearted. I am living my life as one who has been bought with a price. When I find myself in the wilderness, I take hold of my God-given right to speak the Word of the Lord to the devil.*
>
> *And you, Devil, have bound my _____ _____, but I loose _____ right now in the name of Jesus and by the blood of the Lamb. In the name of Jesus Christ, be loosed!*
>
> *Now I thank You, Lord, because it has already transpired in the Spirit. Since the spirit world is more real than the natural world, I rejoice in the Spirit, and I rejoice in the truth, knowing that _____ is free. I have bound the powers of hell, and I have loosed the power of heaven by the authority given to me through the name and shed blood of Jesus Christ, my Lord and Savior.*

The prayer of authority refuses to take *no* for an answer. The Holy Spirit spoke through the psalmist when he declared: "I will declare the decree: the LORD has said unto me, Thou art my Son; this day have I begotten Thee" (Ps. 2:7).

2. Pray the prayer of agreement.

Jesus said in Matthew 18:19–20: "Again I say unto you, That if two of you shall agree on earth as touching any thing that they shall ask, it shall be done for them of my Father which is in heaven. For where two or three are gathered together in my name, there am I in the midst of them."

Pray the prayer of agreement with another believer. We know about the powerful prayer of agreement the disciples prayed in the upper room in Jerusalem. But another powerful prayer of agreement took place as a result of the persecution of believers after Pentecost: "And when they had prayed, the place was shaken where they were assembled together; and they were all filled with the Holy Ghost, and they spake the word of God with boldness" (Acts 4:31).

Our churches need to tap into the power of agreement once again and see the power of God shake them, fill them and anoint them to speak with boldness!

3. Pray the prayer of faith and petition.

In the Gospel of Mark, Jesus declared, "Have faith in God. For verily I say unto you, That whosoever shall say unto this mountain, Be thou removed, and be thou cast into the sea; and shall not doubt in his heart, but shall believe that those things which he saith shall come to pass, he shall have whatsoever he saith" (Mark 11:22–24).

Sometimes we speak to everything except the problem. Perhaps it is time to start speaking to the mountain that is blocking your way.

Brother Norvel Hayes has told me of a conversation he once had with the relatives of a dying man. They approached Brother Hayes and said, "Well, Brother Norvel, we just don't know what else to do. We've done everything we can think of."

"I doubt it," he replied.

They said, "No, we've done everything we know to do. We've had the elders in, we've anointed him with oil, and we've prayed."

Brother Norvel said in his straightforward way, "OK, he's dying of cancer. When was the last time you *screamed* at the cancer?"

"What?"

"When was the last time you talked to the cancer?"

"Well, Brother Hayes, we asked the Lord, and we prayed and..."

"No! When was the last time you *spoke to the cancer?* Look at that mountain in front of you, open up your mouth and begin to declare the Word of the Lord over that mountain!"

Jesus qualified the prayer of faith and petition when He said, "Whosoever shall say unto this mountain, Be thou removed, and be thou cast into the sea; *and shall not doubt in his heart...*" (Mark 11:23, emphasis added). Most of the struggle is going to take place in your mind. Doubt in the mind is something over which you must take authority. Place your spirit back into authority over your soul.

Our problem is that we often listen to our minds instead of to our spirits. We haven't taken every thought into captivity to the obedience of Christ (2 Cor. 10:5). When we listen to our minds, our mouths say what is contrary to the Word of God, and we begin to speak ourselves into demise. No matter how much we may dissect it, examine it or analyze it, prayer demands faith.

One lady in our church prayed and stood by faith for twelve long and lonely years after her drug-addicted husband walked out on her and their three children. She asked God to bring the man back home, and eventually her prayer was answered (even though everyone had thought she was crazy). Twelve years after he had left, he returned home, was delivered from drugs, was restored to his family and began to follow Christ. I actually remarried the couple in my office!

I asked that woman, "How did you hold on for twelve long years?"

She said, "It wasn't hard. For twelve years *I believed I received when I prayed.* No matter what I saw, no matter what I felt like, no matter how much my family said I was crazy, I believed I received when I prayed." That is the prayer of faith and petition.

4. Pray the prayer of thanksgiving, praise and worship.

And they rose early in the morning, and went forth into

82

the wilderness of Tekoa: and as they went forth, Jehoshaphat stood and said, Hear me, O Judah, and ye inhabitants of Jerusalem; Believe in the LORD your God, so shall ye be established; believe his prophets, so shall ye prosper. And when he had consulted with the people, he appointed singers unto the LORD, and that should *praise the beauty of holiness,* as they went out before the army, and to say, *Praise the LORD; for his mercy endureth for ever.* And when they began to sing and to praise, *the LORD set ambushments* against the children of Ammon, Moab, and mount Seir, which were come against Judah; and they were smitten.
—2 CHRONICLES 20:20–22, EMPHASIS ADDED

Several years ago, a young woman in our church was 80 percent deaf in one ear and 100 percent deaf in the other. She was a beautiful girl who faithfully attended every service. She was quick to receive prayer from anyone who was willing— yet her hearing was never restored.

For several years, the homosexual community in Columbus has held a Gay Rights parade. Most of the time our church congregation would attend the event and quietly pray along the parade route in peaceful protest to the homosexual lifestyle.

One particular year I felt we were to do something different. Instead of protesting by waving signs and placards in the traditional manner, we decided to attend the parade and simply line the street on both sides and worship our God in the beauty of holiness.

We were worshiping the Lord as the parade passed by when suddenly I heard somebody squeal just down the line from me. Someone ran up to me and said, "Pastor, come quick, come quick!" I moved through the crowd as quickly as I could while asking, "What happened?"

When I reached the site of the commotion, I noticed the

young lady I just spoke of standing there. When I asked what had happened, the people around her answered, "She can hear! She can hear!" That young lady's hearing was completely and instantly restored as we sang praises to God!

She had been minding her own business, standing there on the sidewalk in Columbus, Ohio when it happened. No one touched her, and no one had directly prayed for her at that time. All she was doing was praising and worshiping her God.

When I asked God how this healing had occurred, He reminded me of a verse in 2 Chronicles 20. He said that when we began to sing praises to Him and worship Him in the beauty of His holiness, He laid ambushments against the enemy (v. 22). Although the armies of the darkened region of the devil's underworld had gathered during that parade, they became so confused in the midst of that blinding praise that they attacked one another as a result of God's ambush and loosed their grip on the girl.

When God sets an ambush, our enemies begin to attack one another!

That's the only girl I know personally who was set free from deafness by a confused demon of homosexuality! I know it sounds odd, but God showed me in the spirit realm that He confused the enemy and caused them to defeat themselves.[5]

Miracles happen when we begin to sing, praise and worship God in unity and joy. When God sets an ambush, our enemies begin to attack one another!

5. Pray the prayer of commitment, consecration and dedication.

The apostle Paul said in Philippians 4:6, "Be anxious for nothing, but in everything by prayer and supplication, with thanksgiving, let your requests be made known to God" (NKJV).

The Bible says in Matthew 26:39, "And [Jesus] went a little farther, and fell on his face, and prayed, saying, O my Father, if it be possible, let this cup pass from me: nevertheless *not as I will, but as thou wilt*" (emphasis added).

I believe my wife, Joni, is one of the greatest examples of someone who daily sets her life apart through the prayer of commitment, consecration and dedication. The word *consecration* describes a setting apart from one thing to something else.[6]

As believers, we need to set ourselves apart from the world and the allure it offers, and to consecrate ourselves unto God. There are so many things vying for our attention, and the Lord is seeking a people whose heart is turned toward Him.

6. Pray in the Spirit, or pray in tongues.

Paul said in 1 Corinthians 14:2–4, "For he that speaketh in an unknown tongue speaketh not unto men, but unto God: for no man understandeth him; howbeit in the spirit he speaketh mysteries. But he that prophesieth speaketh unto men to edification, and exhortation, and comfort. He that speaketh in an unknown tongue edifieth himself; but he that prophesieth edifieth the church." In the Book of Jude we are told, "But ye, beloved, building up yourselves on your most holy faith, praying in the Holy Ghost..." (Jude 20).

Don't be fooled by the efforts of misinformed teachers who say that Paul encouraged people *not* to speak in tongues in his letters to the Corinthians. The truth is that he *encouraged* people to speak in tongues, but he asked that they do it decently and in order when in public meetings.

7. Pray the prayer of intercession.

The Bible says in Romans 8:26–27, 34:

> Likewise the Spirit also helpeth our infirmities: for we know not what we should pray for as we ought: but *the Spirit itself maketh intercession for us* with groanings

which cannot be uttered. And he that searcheth the hearts knoweth what is the mind of the Spirit, because *he maketh intercession for the saints* according to the will of God...Who is he that condemneth? It is Christ that died, yea rather, that is risen again, who is even at the right hand of God, *who also maketh intercession for us.*

—EMPHASIS ADDED

The highest form of prayer you will ever pray occurs when you surrender to the prayer of the Spirit of God who dwells in your heart. This usually moves beyond prayer in your native language and even beyond prayer in your prayer language or "unknown tongues" into what the Bible calls "groanings which cannot be uttered" (Rom. 8:26). This type of prayer is intercession; it is standing in the gap for people.

Hannah, a godly woman who lived hundreds of years before Jesus was born, appears to have entered this level of intercession even before the advent of the Holy Spirit. (See 1 Samuel 1:10–15.) Hannah was barren and was praying for a child. She reached the point before the Lord where she couldn't even frame her prayer in words. She was so overwhelmed with the passion of birthing her dream that the Spirit of God had to take over and pray through her. The prophet Samuel, her son, entered the world as a result of her Spirit-breathed intercessory prayers.

Prayer is as important to our spirits as breathing is to our physical bodies.

If you ever reach that point where the Spirit of God so fills you that He Himself is praying through you, you will experience great success. You will be praying God's will, in perfection and purity by the Spirit.

If you are confused by all of this, let Paul settle the matter for you. The great apostle said it bluntly and yet eloquently: "I thank my God, I speak with tongues more than ye all: Yet in the church I had rather speak five words with my understanding, that by my voice I might teach others also" (1 Cor. 14:18–19).

PRAYER IS NOT AN OPTION

Prayer is as important to our spirits as breathing is to our physical bodies. Prayer is not an option—it is mandatory for anyone who would please God and live a godly life. The apostle of prayer, E. M. Bounds, one of the great leaders God anointed to redig the rejuvenating well of effectual, fervent prayer, said it this way:

> Nothing is more important to God than prayer in dealing with mankind. But is it likewise all-important to man to pray. Failure to pray is failure along the whole line of life. It is failure of duty, service and spiritual progress. God must help man by prayer. He who does not pray, therefore, robs himself of God's help and places God where he cannot help man. Man must pray to God if love for God is to exist.[7]

The Mountain
and the Seed

Chapter 6

*And Jesus answering saith unto them, Have
faith in God. For verily I say unto you, That
whosoever shall say unto this mountain, Be thou
removed, and be thou cast into the sea; and
shall not doubt in his heart, but shall believe
that those things which he saith shall come to
pass; he shall have whatsoever he saith.*
—MARK 11:22–23

There is one ancient well the devil hopes we will never redig in our generation. It is one of our fathers' wells that he fears the most. The water from this well transforms the conquered into conquerors and the fearful into the fearless. It is the key that places all of the resources and power of heaven into the frailest of human hands. My friend, I want to drink deeply from this ancient well of my fathers: the well of faith.

God has used many people in the area of faith throughout human history, but He called one man in particular from the plumber's trade to plumb the depths of the ancient well of faith. We know this is true because of the supernatural fruit of faith in his ministry.

Smith Wigglesworth was a blue-collar worker, a servant of God who would read only the Bible and who dared to believe and act upon the things that God said while others gave them only lip service.

Many have read the account of how Wigglesworth once walked into the parlor of a funeral home where the body of a man had lain for three days. He was on a mission from God. He abruptly told the family to get out of the room. Then he grabbed the man by the lapels and pulled him out of the casket! That wasn't enough. He propped up the man's body against the wall and commanded it, "Live!"

When he released the man's body, the stiffened corpse promptly fell on the floor with a thud. That is probably where you and I would have quit, but most of us don't have the kind of faith that Wigglesworth had!

Wigglesworth grabbed the lapels of the coat on the corpse and propped the body against the wall once more. Again he shouted, "I told you once, now I tell you again...*live!*"

Again, the stiffened corpse fell to the floor with the same thud it had made the first time. Who knows what in creation that poor family and funeral home workers must have been thinking with all the noise coming from behind that closed door!

A third time Smith Wigglesworth picked up the corpse and propped it against the wall. He pointed his finger at the body and demanded, "I've told you once, I've told you twice, but I shan't tell you again after this third time. Now, *live!*"

Suddenly the man coughed, shook his head, wiped off his face and walked out of that funeral home!

This supernatural raising of the dead took place in Smith Wigglesworth's ministry not once, not twice, but *fourteen times.* Some say it was even more. Wigglesworth had the God kind of faith to command the dead to come back to life again. Have you ever seen someone raised from the dead? If your answer is *no,* may I ask you, "Have you ever prayed for it?"

FAITH COMES THREE WAYS

How do we get this amazing kind of faith? For that matter, how do we get any kind of faith?

The Bible says that faith comes three ways:

1. God gives unto every man the measure of faith that he needs (Rom. 12:3).

2. Faith comes by hearing the Word of God (Rom. 10:17).

3. Faith comes to us by divine delivery through impartation, as Paul shares in his letter to Timothy:

> When I call to remembrance the *unfeigned faith* that is in thee, which dwelt first in thy grandmother Lois, and thy mother Eunice; and I am persuaded that in thee also. Wherefore I put thee in remembrance that thou stir up *the gift of God, which is in thee by the putting on of my hands.*
>
> —2 TIMOTHY 1:5–6, EMPHASIS ADDED

Before Smith Wigglesworth went to heaven, he wrapped his huge plumber's arms around Lester Sumrall and prayed over him, "Let the faith that is in me come into this young man." This is especially meaningful to me because on the very last occasion Dr. Lester Sumrall stood on the platform of World Harvest Church in Columbus, Ohio, none of us knew that he would soon be gone. Although he was the picture of health, his time was near.

That day Dr. Sumrall suddenly called me to the front of the congregation, wrapped his arms around me in much the same manner as Wigglesworth had done to him and prayed, "Let the faith that is in me come into this man."

I desire to pass this impartation of faith on to you.

Let it come, Lord Jesus, even as we join our hearts and minds through the pages of this book. By Your Spirit, rend the dividing lines of time and distance, open the gates of heaven and pour out supernatural faith upon Your people. Let an impartation come into our spirits from the well of our fathers so that when we speak a thing according to Your will, it shall be established. Let Your faith, Lord God, be imparted to every willing heart in the name of Jesus.

I challenge you to take the next few minutes and declare to the Lord what you are believing in faith to receive. Then praise Him because you know it is already on the way!

FAITH CAN BE NULLIFIED BY RELIGIOUS TRADITION

Faith is a precious gift from God, but *it is a gift that can be lost or nullified!* I didn't say it—Jesus did. He rebuked the Pharisees and religious leaders in His day saying, "Thus have ye made the commandment of God of *none effect* by your *tradition*" (Matt. 15:6, emphasis added).

Tradition may steal your faith in three ways:

1. Tradition *takes doubt to school and produces unbelief.* The Spirit of God still moves freely even when there is doubt, because doubt is nothing more than questioning. Yet even Jesus found it harder to work miracles in the presence of unbelief. (See Matthew 13:58.) Doubt says, "I *wonder* if it could be," but unbelief declares, "I *know* it cannot be." Tradition will school you in the art of producing unbelief.

2. Tradition makes the Word of God of no effect by training you *to ignore the power of Satan, to trivialize the spirit of the antichrist and to*

94

be ignorant of your own power. When we por-
tray the archangel of hell, the chief of demons,
as wearing a laughable red suit with horns and
a forked tail, he doesn't mind at all! He knows
that to refuse to acknowledge the existence of
a literal, utterly evil devil is the first step to
refusing to acknowledge the existence of a literal God. The Word of God specifically forbids
men to trivialize demonic power.[1]

3. Tradition *steals your faith and hope;* it refuses
to allow you to stand up in the winter of your
life and bear fruit as if it were springtime.
Tradition will train you in the art of being a
weak, ineffectual Christian. Tradition refuses
to allow you to call those things that be not as
though they were. It refuses to allow you to
offer the sacrifice of praise, giving thanks to
God even when you are experiencing pain and
sorrow.

In the darkness of your despair, when everyone around you
says you should cave in and give up, true faith rises up on the
inside of you and declares, "I am going to be resurrected even
though everything looks hopeless!"

GET RADICAL, "PROMISED-LAND" FAITH

Faith transforms the way you pray. It energizes and empowers
the way you do battle in the heavenly realm. When faith takes
hold in the redeemed human spirit, walls come down!
Suddenly our words take on creative capability. We find that
when we declare a thing in the Spirit, God establishes it. If
faith is rising in your heart as you read these words, begin to
declare your miracle. Open up your mouth and speak creative
words with the anointing of God.

Get radical, "promised-land" faith! Begin to proclaim salvation over your family, and ask the Holy Spirit to begin to soften their hearts toward the things of God. Speak to your bank account and command it to prosper. Speak to your car—command it to operate as it should and to keep from breaking down. Speak to your spirit and declare yourself to be holy, pure and righteous in Christ Jesus. Declare that you have wisdom because He has been made wisdom to you. Declare that you will increase in wisdom and favor with God and with men.

When faith takes hold in the redeemed human spirit, walls come down!

Most people don't have a future, because they have no hope; they only have a prolonged today. They live in what I call the "someday syndrome." In order to have something you've never had before, you must do something different than what you are doing right now. God-given hope sees your tomorrows as different from your today!

Do you know that God has given you the power to establish your world within the boundaries of His Word? You create your world by declaring the Word of God into your future by faith!

Faith Requires Obedience

The only way to operate in faith is to walk in faith. Smith Wigglesworth paid a dear price to redig the well of faith, and opposition came from virtually every angle.

Kenneth E. Hagin tells the story of the time God spoke to Smith Wigglesworth to "go raise Lazarus." This particular "Lazarus" was a Welsh tin miner who used to work in the mines during the day and preach the gospel at night. However, he had contracted tuberculosis. This man had spent six years as an invalid by the time Mr. Wigglesworth received the orders from God to seek him out.

Wigglesworth wrote down on a postcard what the Lord had said and mailed it to the miner's home before his visit. When he arrived, he was greeted at the door by a man holding the card.

"Did you send this?" the man asked. "Do you think we believe in this? Here, take it!" And he threw it at Wigglesworth's feet.

Then the man called a servant and said, "Take this man and show him Lazarus." He said to Wigglesworth, "The moment you see him, you will be ready to go home."[2]

If natural appearances could be trusted, the cynical man was also a prophet. When Smith Wigglesworth was introduced to Lazarus, all he saw was a mass of skin and bones. The man had been spoon-fed his meals for six years, but, even as bad as the illness was, the state of his faith was worse than the state of his physical body.

Most of us would have taken the cynic's advice, given our condolences and headed for home. Mr. Wigglesworth didn't have that option because he had heard from God. Faith doesn't give up and it doesn't give in—it prevails. He greeted Lazarus and left the house, but he would soon return.

Mr. Wigglesworth sought out seven other people to stand with him in prayer that night. After praying and fasting all night, he showed up at Lazarus' house with his seven prayer warriors the following morning. They were greeted by the same cynical family member who had greeted Mr. Wigglesworth the day before.

What happened next also shows us that faith requires us to walk with listening and obedient hearts.

While Wigglesworth had been fasting, God had told him what to do: "Don't pray, don't anoint him with oil, don't touch him. All eight of you gather around the bed, hold hands and repeat the name of Jesus."

So he said, "We just stood around the bed and said, 'Jesus,

Jesus, Jesus (all eight of them in unison), Jesus, Jesus!'"

As they spoke, the power of God fell. Then it lifted like a

Faith requires obedience to activate God's provision.

cloud. They continued to hold hands and say, "Jesus, Jesus," as the power kept coming down and lifting. The sixth time it came down, Lazarus said, "I've been bitter in my heart, and I know I have grieved the

Spirit of God." He repented and cried out, "O God, let this be to Thy glory." As he said that, the power of God went through him, and he was healed.

Lazarus got up and dressed himself without any assistance. Then he and Brother Wigglesworth walked downstairs while singing the Doxology.[3] Lazarus testified in an open-air meeting about what God had done, and many were saved.[4]

Faith requires obedience to activate God's provision. Most of the miracles that occurred in Dr. Lester Sumrall's life and ministry began with a divine seed of direction, but they required a giant step of faith to yield a harvest.

Dr. Sumrall described the way he purchased his first television station in the book *Secrets of Answered Prayer*:

> When God brought me back from the Orient, He told me, "Lester Sumrall, I want you to win a million souls."
>
> I said, "Lord, how can I see that come to pass?"
>
> He told me, "Get on television."
>
> I'll admit I was fearful, so I started with a little radio station. It was successful. One day I met a man in Washington, D.C., who asked me, "Do you want a TV station?"
>
> "Yes, sir."
>
> "Well, I've got one for sale in Indianapolis."
>
> "I'd buy it, but I don't have even ten dollars to spare."
>
> In a total miracle transaction, he sold me the station for a million dollars, when I didn't have any money. But

I signed for it on faith. Within a week, through a number of extraordinary transactions, even the amount owed was cut in half. The purchase of our South Bend, Indiana, station was just as miraculous as the first one. Through the miracle action of prayer, I went on the air to reach and win the million people for Christ that God desired of me.[5]

We've seen how God worked through the faith and obedience of men like Smith Wigglesworth and Dr. Lester Sumrall. The Bible says that God is no respecter of persons (Acts 10:34). In other words, He doesn't play favorites. He will do for you what He did for both of those men.

All it takes is a seed of faith and the courage to plant it in the field of impossibility. Are you ready? Then take a deep drink from the ancient well of faith and live!

The Divine "Go"

Chapter 7

*Go ye into all the world, and preach the gospel
to every creature.*
—MARK 16:15

N early two thousand years ago, one hundred twenty
disciples dared to obey the last words Jesus spoke on
this earth. They secluded themselves in a second-
story room and fasted and prayed until a gale-force wind of
the Holy Spirit picked them up and scattered them to the four
corners of the globe. (See the Book of Acts.) Within twenty
years they and others caught up in God's whirlwind had
evangelized the entire known world.

They didn't have a Bible. They didn't have an ink pen, a
printing press or a computer (let alone mailing lists). They
didn't have a radio or television studio or a nice church building with a state-of-the-art sound system. They weren't members of a denomination or even a structured organization. *All*

they had was a divine mandate to go.

"Go ye into all the world, and preach the gospel to every creature" (Mark 16:15). That is the first mission of every Christian and of every gathering of Christian believers. For most of us, it is also our first failure in the faith.

Do you know how the Gospel of Mark—the action Gospel—ends? Mark writes, "And they went forth, and preached every where, the Lord working with them, and confirming the word with signs following. Amen" (Mark 16:20).

How does your personal gospel end?

God works with you and confirms the Word with signs following *only* when you go (Mark 16:20). I'm also convinced that God blesses nothing that is sedentary. Merriam-Webster's Collegiate Dictionary defines *sedentary* as "doing or requiring much sitting; permanently attached." Unfortunately, too many American Christians seem to be permanently attached to what they sit on in church services week after week!

In the 1800s, the century after the American colonies declared independence and became a nation, God raised up the son of a poor Scotsman to redig the holy well of missions in Christ's name. David Livingstone ultimately became one of the greatest missionary evangelists that ever walked the face of the earth.

"THE SPIRIT OF MISSIONS IS THE SPIRIT OF THE MASTER"

Dr. Livingstone's most famous statement to the sedentary church of his generation was: *"God had only one Son, and He made that Son a missionary."* Livingstone devoted the rest of his life to demonstrating what God can do through someone who will say *yes* to Him and become a missionary to the lost.

If you wonder what qualified David Livingstone to say what he said, consider his track record in Christ. Born in

1813 to a poor Scottish family, he made his way from a job in a cotton mill to medical school and then on to the mission field. His life was characterized by tenacity, hard work and perseverance in the face of impossible odds.

This doctor, missionary, geographer and explorer was convinced that *the spirit of missions is the spirit of the Master.* He decided to make his home in the uncharted and largely unexplored interior of Africa that was called "the White Man's Graveyard."

This adventurer for God would not take *no* for an answer or settle for less than what he believed the Lord was asking of him. Livingstone was ahead of his time because he sought to win *entire people groups* to the Lord rather than simply concentrate on individual conversions. He believed entire villages, tribes and cultures would be receptive to the gospel if they came into contact with pure Christian truth and principles.

ONLY THE BEGINNING OF THE MISSIONARY ENTERPRISE

Much of the world learned about Dr. Livingstone through his efforts to explore, chart and open up the vast interior regions of the "Dark Continent" to the rest of the world. But in Livingstone's view, his exploration was merely a means to a greater and eternal end. He made his true purpose clear when he said, "The end of the geographical feat is only the beginning of the missionary enterprise."[1]

Dr. Livingstone forged ahead through Africa's jungles and deserts, accompanied only by tribesmen, making a way for the unreached people of Africa's interior to be reached with the gospel. He believed that God had called him to open up Africa to Christian missions, and he devoted all of his energies to that calling. He did it with a determination and steadfastness that many of us have never seen, proclaiming, *"I will place no value on anything I have, or may possess, except in relation to the kingdom of Christ."* [2]

The world often waited for years at a time for word from this famed missionary struggling in obscurity to bring light to the Dark Continent. The stories of his exploration spurred men and women of God to lay down their lives on behalf of the people of Africa.

Despite almost impossible odds, Dr. Livingstone was known for his consistent efforts to send regular reports of his progress to the outside world. When he seemed to disappear in East Africa for almost three years, the Royal Geographical Society of England prepared an expedition to find him. The effort was called off after a few letters finally arrived.

"DR. LIVINGSTONE, I PRESUME"

The publisher of the *New York Herald* wanted more proof, so he commissioned an English explorer and naturalized American named Henry Morton Stanley to "find Livingstone." Many people can still quote the famous phrase, "Dr. Livingstone, I presume," taken from Stanley's account of his meeting with Dr. Livingstone on the east shore of Lake Tanganyika in 1871.[3]

God gave the church power to go, not to say *no*.

The sedentary spirit that plagued the church of David Livingston's day still permeates the church in this country today. When anything (be it natural or spiritual) becomes sedentary, atrophy sets in. Atrophy is a wasting away of vitality, strength and potential. Muscles that atrophy shrivel up and ultimately cease to function. As the popular saying goes, "Use it or lose it." God gave the church power to go, not to say *no*.

The only way the church can remain strong is for it to exercise its faith and considerable collections of spiritual gifts. God makes us strong as we move and encounter resistance in obedience to His command. When we sit, we waste.

A sedentary church is a bored church without vision, anticipation, faith or good fruit. It is characterized by Christians who grow more spiritually obese and self-centered with every month that passes.

In contrast, the Father and Author of the church is a "missionary God." His Word, the Bible, is a "missions Book" from cover to cover. (If you doubt me, take a few minutes to read Matthew 28, Mark 16 and the first two chapters of the Book of Acts.)

IT PAYS TO GO

The Bible is a missionary Book because throughout its pages people are *going*. The most notable time you see a great leader staying someplace instead of going is when King David decided not to go to war with his troops. We all know what happened next—he stayed when he should have gone, so he looked where he should not have been looking. David's act of adultery with Bathsheba and the cold-blooded murder of her husband were the result. It pays to go instead of saying *no*.

The movers and shakers of the Bible were never stationary or sedentary. They were always going and moving on in the plan of God. You can almost hear the Father describing the mission of His Son, Jesus:

> I only had one Son, and I sent Him as a missionary beyond His comfort zone far from the pavilions of glory. He left His first estate to be born as a humble babe and to live as a mortal man. He ate what He wasn't used to eating; He wore what He wasn't used to wearing. The Creator submitted Himself to that which He had created. I sent Him to a people who were not His people and asked Him to make them His own. Then He restored them to Me through His own blood, through

His death and final resurrection. "This is my beloved Son, in whom I am well pleased" (Matt. 3:17).

God is a missionary God. The Bible is a missionary Book. The church is a missionary institution. Search the Book of Acts—nowhere will you find an appeal for people to "come to church." They were all so busy doing the work of the kingdom that they knew they could not forsake the assembling of themselves together. They needed the strength and encouragement Christian fellowship provided.

These people had been fighting demons all day—and not from a frightened or defensive posture. Their battle scars weren't on their backsides from running and defending themselves. They won their commendation scars while hammering at the gates of hell, beating up the devil's minions and snatching souls from the flames of Hell!

Jesus put the focus on His sacrificial service to others.

Let me say it again. God is a missionary God! The Bible is a missionary Book! The church is a missionary institution, and the gospel is a missionary message!

T. L. Osborne, a great patriarch in the faith, has said for fifty years, "Why should anybody have the opportunity to hear the gospel twice before everybody has had the opportunity to hear the gospel once?" He is another man whom God anointed to redig the well of missions in Christ's name.

The church is a missionary institution, but if it becomes introverted or turns inward, then, like an ingrown toenail, it gets sore, becomes infected and produces a terrible stench. The church must always look outward, sending out missionaries in Christ's name. Anything less is disobedience to God.

JESUS PUT THE FOCUS ON SACRIFICIAL SERVICE

What did Jesus' mission cost Him? We look at His ministry

and see the grand scope of His power, His miracles and His ultimate triumph. Jesus put the focus on His sacrificial service to others. The Bible says:

> And whosoever of you will be the chiefest, shall be servant of all. For even the Son of man came not to be ministered unto, but to minister [to serve and wait on], and to give his life a ransom for many.
>
> —MARK 10:44–45, EMPHASIS ADDED

The Bible does not say, "Close yourself off from the rest of the world, attend grand conferences and gather unto yourself a mountain of tapes, books, videos and CDs. Accumulate knowledge of Me, but do nothing to win the lost in My name." Instead it says:

> Go ye therefore, and teach all nations, baptizing them in the name of the Father, and of the Son, and of the Holy Ghost: Teaching them to observe all things whatsoever I have commanded you: and, lo, I am with you alway, even unto the end of the world. Amen.
>
> —MATTHEW 28:19–20

Our prayer must become, "Make me like Jesus, Holy Spirit. Conform me to the image of Your Son, Father." It is the only way to fulfill our destiny, whether it takes us upstairs to our teenager's room, next door to share God's love with our neighbor or across the ocean to Bombay, Budapest or Brasilia.

GOD MIGHT ANSWER YOUR PRAYER TO BE LIKE JESUS!

I'm afraid that most of us don't ask to be like Jesus because we are afraid God might actually answer that prayer! The truth is that we don't do what Jesus did because we won't do what Jesus did. We don't fast for forty days—most of us can't even fast four hours without getting a "Mac attack"! We get angry with God, the preacher and our dog when the Sunday morning church service goes past noon.

We need to take on ourselves the mind of Christ, the One who gave Himself as a ransom for many. I had the privilege of traveling all over the Orient with Dr. Sumrall as he ministered to massive crowds numbering in the tens of thousands. He used to stand on a platform and say, "Look at my face! You are an Oriental by accident. I am an Oriental by choice! I left my home and abandoned my livelihood to come to you! I didn't even want to come, but He sent me. Now I have come with a message from the King! Jesus loves you and gave His life as a ransom for many."

The worldwide mission of the church of Jesus Christ is embodied in the Incarnation. If you want to understand what God has really called you to do as an individual, and what He has called the church to do corporately, then you must first come to grips with the fact that God's purposes are wrapped up in the Incarnation.

The Incarnation is the methodology by which God became a man. Jesus is Emmanuel, "God with us." (See Matthew 1:23.) God wrapped Himself in flesh and blood and gave Himself as a gift to mankind. Why? He was on a mission to seek and save those who were lost (Luke 19:10). He gave His life as a ransom for many (Matt. 20:28; Mark 10:45).

Too Many of Us Shrink From Sacrifice

When you named the name of Christ, He put His brand on you. He marked you for life and said, "My purpose has now become your purpose." Now, you and I are called to seek and save that which was lost and to give our lives as a ransom for many. The problem is that too many of us shrink away from sacrifice in any form.

When we look at the Incarnation, we see the mission of God, which has now become our mission. Have you noticed that every believer who is really saved feels the urge to preach at one time or another? Every preacher who is honest with you will admit that he or she felt a desire to go to the world at some point. If the world is not in your heart, then God is not in your heart!

Does that mean that everyone is called to be a missionary to a foreign country? No, but it does mean that everyone must either go or be personally involved in helping others go. Why should a local church in America be involved in **We have no reason or right to be bored in our Christianity. We have a whole world for which to pray.** Sunday school, in Little League teams, in outreach efforts to children in inner-city projects? Our mission from God is to seek them, to save them and to give our lives for them. Who knows? There might be another David Livingstone in that Sunday school class, playing second base or watching a puppet show on the littered sidewalk.

We have no reason or right to be bored in our Christianity. We have a whole world for which to pray. Jesus came and fulfilled His mission. Just before He returned to the portals of glory with His Father, He said to His disciples, "As my Father hath sent me, even so send I you" (John 20:21).

No believer is exempt from that divine mandate!

EXERT THE POWER OF CHRIST AND INFLUENCE THE WORLD

This mandate colors everything we do at World Harvest Church. We even encourage the senior class at our preparatory school to keep the Great Commission a priority when planning their senior trips each year. Will they go to the Bahamas to soak up the sun on beautiful white sands, or will they journey to Washington, D.C. and exert the power of

Christ in the nation's seat of power, which in turn influences the world?

Once you understand the incarnation of Christ in your heart, once the Great Commission becomes your own commission, it will change your prayer life and the way you view your work in the local church. Suddenly, you realize you aren't merely working for the church; you are working in the kingdom of God.

As a kingdom worker with a great commission, you must learn to pray in the Holy Spirit. Brother Sumrall was once in the mountains of Tibet, riding on a donkey, when he fell off onto the ground. Scarlet fever had attacked his body, and he lay there at the point of death. Then suddenly his eyes opened, and the fever left him.

Much later a letter came to him from a little grandmother who lived halfway around the world in South Bend, Indiana. She said that she had been praying for a little missionary boy in his twenties at such and such a time. She wrote: "God awakened me from my bed and caused me to pray and rebuke fever from your body. I just wanted you to know God is looking out for you." When Dr. Sumrall did all of the time calculations, he discovered that God had spoken to this little grandmother intercessor at exactly the same time he was near death on that Tibetan hillside![4]

BE QUICK TO OBEY AND PRAY

When was the last time God woke you from a sound sleep to pray for someone? Be quick to obey—it may be your crucial part to play in the Great Commission of Christ.

We are the generation destined for the manifestation and revelation of the glory of God. That means we're going to both see it and understand it!

You and I have a fresh mandate from God to redig the well of our fathers called missions. We have been personally chosen, trained and equipped to play a part in changing our world for Christ. Does the world need us? Consider just a few of the following facts and answer the question for yourself:

The Netherlands, population 15,982,000—born-again believers, 21 percent.[5] With the history of a glorious Christian nation, the Netherlands has suffered a great social breakdown. The enemy has attacked by replacing Christianity with the permissive lifestyle of sexual immorality, causing the number of believers to drop nearly 200,000 souls a year.

Suriname, population 434,000—born-again believers, 25 percent.[6] Left in the wake of great struggle, the post-independent state of this nation is disastrous and devoid of peace. Christian leaders of the faith are rare.

Ireland, population 3,841,000—born-again believers, 1 percent.[7] The religious establishment accounts for 85 percent of the population.[8] Multiple generations of spiritual blindness plague the people who know a "kind of gospel, but lack the power thereof."

Canada, population 31,593,000—born-again believers, 40 percent.[9] The Christian church in Canada is currently suffering great losses. With a lack of vision and evangelism, it is losing many to compromise in alternative lifestyles. The loss of biblical roots has put Canada in a great need for revival.

Germany, population 83,029,000—born-again believers, 38 percent.[10] With the collapse of communism, the opportunity for growth is tremendous in this country, but once again, the workers are few. With Germany in a quick economic rebound, there is a divine opportunity to transform it into a nation after God.

Brazil, population 174,469,000—born-again believers, 22 percent.[11] The youth of Brazil are under a demonic attack of massive proportions. With over 8 million people living in the streets and sewers, the enemy is seeking to destroy the next generation of Brazilians through drugs, prostitution and

AIDS. The church is growing at a rapid rate, but help for the children is scarce.

Australia, population 19,400,000—born-again believers, 24 percent.[12] Secularism has taken the place of faith, and the strength of the church is on a dramatic decline. With missions to this region sinking to a low ebb, support is needed to bring Jesus to a blind but searching people.

Russia, population 145,400,000 million—born-again believers 2 percent.[13, 14] In a nation born in tyranny, martyrs from Russia number in the millions. Ninety percent of all church buildings were seized or destroyed when communist persecution ran rampant. However, since the rise of democracy in 1991, Russia has had great open doors for ministers of the Good News, and the people now have an enormous interest in religion.

Japan, population 126,800,000—born-again believers, 1 percent.[15, 16] With over 80 percent of the people of Japan practicing atheists, unresponsiveness to the gospel has frozen growth and quenched the Holy Spirit. As a central destination to missionaries around the world, spiritual warfare is being waged on the grandest of scales. Missionaries are looking for the power of God to break through any day.

Mexico, population 101,879,000—born-again believers, 6 percent.[17] The religious establishment has over 85 percent of Mexico's citizens held in spiritual blindness. With poverty, national debt and inflation at all-time highs, this nation needs a Redeemer. Revival is taking place in this region and throughout Central America as denominations are combining forces and praying down strongholds.

Jamaica, population 2,665,000—born-again believers, 61 percent.[18] Although a nation of great beauty, as a coastal island, Jamaica is plagued by drug trafficking and Mafia powers. As a leader in the Caribbean, the spiritual climate of this nation affects many of the surrounding areas. With such great influence, Jamaica is a prime target for revival.

Kenya, population nearly 30,000,000—born-again believers, 38 percent.[19] Because Kenya is a key nation in Africa, the enemy savagely contests every advance of the gospel. Widespread evangelism and worldwide focus assure great progress will be soon to come. Still, there are not enough workers equipped to handle an outpouring of God.

Estonia, population 1,423,000—born-again believers, 40 percent.[20] God is moving in a mighty way among the youth of Estonia, with 90 percent of the nation's children attending Sunday school regularly. God is raising up a generation with a desire to seek after Him. Still, leadership trainers and educators are desperately needed to continue to push forward.

The Bahamas, population 298,000—born-again believers, 73 percent.[21] New tourism and trade have polluted this beautiful country with materialism and drug addiction. Still, the gospel is spreading. Actually, all of the Caribbean nations are hot spots for new and great moves of the Holy Spirit and are in great need of help.

Sometimes the mandate of God to "go" takes you into some of the strangest places and situations. We, in fact, found ourselves working with a ministry reaching out to people involved in a form of human slavery. That ministry would be very near and dear to the heart of Dr. David Livingstone, were he still alive. His work not only opened the way for missionaries to preach the gospel to the interior regions of Africa, but it also helped abolish the slave trade in that continent. In the last year of his life he wrote to his daughter:

> No one can estimate the amount of God-pleasing good that will be done, if, by Divine favor, this awful slave-trade, into the midst of which I have come, be abolished. This will be something to have lived for, and the conviction has grown in my mind that it was for this end I have been detained so long.[22]

A Million Murdered and 100,000 Enslaved by Muslim Extremists

For the past fifteen years, one of the largest civil wars in the history of the world has been raging in the African nation of Sudan. Over one million people are dead, and in the twenty-first century alone, thousands of men and women have been carried away and sold in the open markets as slaves by a radical extremist Muslim government.

Throughout this fifteen-year period, churches have been raided and burned to the ground. Young women have been stripped, repeatedly raped, mutilated and paraded around by Muslim extremists as trophies to demonstrate their exploits. Christian men over the age of eighteen have had their hands and arms chopped off with machetes to mark them for the rest of their lives as "infidels." Their only crime was that they went to church, lifted their hands and said, "I believe in Jesus Christ."

> **We are a mighty, marching force for righteousness in the earth, and we have a solemn responsibility under God to stand up and be heard, and to rise and go when God says go.**

The church in America was fairly oblivious to this carnage until a band of demonized Muslim extremists flew two aircraft into the Twin Towers in New York City. Then America quickly put down her foot and sent troops around the world, saying, "We expect you to help us do something about this because several thousand of our own innocent people have just been slaughtered!"

Ironically, just a few weeks before the Twin Towers collapsed, the United Nations voted with one voice to remove the United States from its Human Rights Commission. The U.S. was replaced with the African nation of Sudan, ruled by the same extremist Muslim regime that has slaughtered more than a million of its own citizens simply because they profess to be Christians! Secretary of State Colin Powell once told a House committee, "There is perhaps no greater tragedy on the face of the earth today than the tragedy that is unfolding in the Sudan."[23]

How could this be? American senators and congressmen told me the reason they hadn't done anything for fifteen years was because no one in the Christian community spoke out loudly enough. They realized, however, that once so many people began to learn of this terrible situation, they were going to have to take action.

Don't ever let the devil dupe you into believing that you can't do something about wrongs perpetrated against the church or against Christians, regardless of their nationality. We are a mighty, marching force for righteousness in the earth, and we have a solemn responsibility under God to stand up and be heard, and to rise and go when God says go.

Former Secretary of State Madeleine Albright, who served under former President Bill Clinton, once made the stunning statement to a group of religious leaders, "The human rights situation in Sudan is not marketable to the American people."[24] I'm sorry, but when we get to heaven, there are going to be a million Christians who will look at us and ask, "How could you have forgotten us?"

So, what has our ministry done about this situation? We are putting our money where our mouth is. We discovered that we can buy back the freedom of the survivors of this holocaust who were put into slavery for their faith. As a result, we are purchasing the freedom of Christian men, women and children who have been held by Muslims. Many of these freed slaves bear the savage marks of mutilation inflicted on them, identifying them as Christians for the rest of their lives.

"I SAW A MAN ON A TRUCK LOADED WITH MONEY"

I received a letter from a young woman who was a practicing attorney in her thirties. She had left her law practice to attend World Harvest Bible College, but I had lost track of her.

She said, "Pastor, I have to tell you a story. I was in the middle of the desert in Sudan with Senator Sam Brownback of Kansas when I saw a man on top of a truck that was loaded with money. I watched this man give piles of money to an African man, and then I watched him go to a long line of slaves in chains. As he unlocked their chains, he said these words: 'I set you free in the name of Jesus Christ...with funds provided by the body of Christ through World Harvest Church and the Breakthrough ministry.'"

> **You have a divine mandate and a holy commission to go into all the world and preach the gospel.**

She said, "I ran up to him and asked, 'What did you say?'" After he repeated his words, she told him, "I went to Bible college there."

It turned out that this young woman, a World Harvest Bible College graduate, was a human rights advocate from Senator Brownback's office, lobbying in the United States Senate on behalf of the Sudanese slaves.

When I went to Washington, D.C., virtually every person seemed to know this young lady. Never underestimate the power of God to move you where He wants you if you dare to say *yes!*

The work continues to expand in Sudan. As of this writing, we've set free more than 15,700 men and women, spending nearly half a million dollars in the process.

Now is the time for you and me to take our place as God's chosen people. He has blessed us with freedom, wealth and abundance so that we might be a blessing. The lost and bound are calling to us. We hold the keys to their prison cells.

You possess the Word of Life and the power of binding and loosing in Jesus' name. (See Matthew 16:19). You have a divine mandate and a holy commission to go into all the world and preach the gospel.

DARE TO PRAY THIS PRAYER

Regardless of where you will be a month or a year from now, dare to pray this prayer with me right now:

> *Father, I present myself as a living sacrifice to You. As You sent the Lord Jesus Christ, so have You commissioned me to seek and save that which was lost and to give my life for the sake of the gospel.*
>
> *There is no sacrifice too great, no duty too small for me to perform when I picture You on the cross, Lord. Grant me the grace and power to serve with a willing heart, whether You send me to clean toilets in a church building, to preach the gospel on the streets and in the parks of my city or to lay down my life in service to the lost in another nation.*
>
> *Whatever You send me to do, I will do with my whole heart, mind, soul and strength. I am a bond-servant bought with Your own blood. I give you my life, my strength, my desires, my future, my past, my present. Take me and send me where You will.*
>
> *In Jesus' name I pray, amen.*

Troubled Waters

Chapter **8**

Lord, if thou wilt, thou canst make me clean.
And Jesus put forth his hand, and touched him,
saying, I will; be thou clean.
—MATTHEW 8:2–3

Ahundred years ago, tuberculosis was running rampant throughout the United States, and smallpox epidemics had brought entire cities to their knees. The numbers of the dead and dying became so overwhelming that Americans were forced to order caskets from other nations just to bury the dead.

During this bleak time, the voice of a businessman rang out strong and true. He was preaching from Acts 10:38, where Luke described: "How God anointed Jesus of Nazareth with the Holy Ghost and with power: who went about doing good, and healing all that were oppressed of the devil; for God was with him."

John G. Lake was a highly successful Illinois businessman,

but he came from a family immersed in disease, tragedy and death. Eight family members died during a thirty-two-year period, and at least one family member was an invalid throughout those dark years.

In the foreword to a book titled *The Astounding Diary of Dr. John G. Lake,* one editor described the dismal background of the Lake family:

> A shroud of sickness pervaded the atmosphere around the family as an endless train of doctors, nurses, hospitals, hearses, funerals, graveyards and tombstones cast their ugly shadows over their lives.[1]

Young Mr. Lake had been taught by his church that the time of miracles was over and that God no longer healed people today. His wife was dying of tuberculosis, and although he took her to church every Sunday, she continued to grow weaker each day. He finally discovered the *truth about healing* while praying for her and reading God's Word.

In his desperation, John G. Lake reread Acts 10:38, and for the first time the light of God's Word gave him a new understanding. He saw that Jesus was *anointed with the Holy Spirit and with power* before He went about doing good and healing all.

Then Lake read in Mark 16:17–18 that *those who believe* will "lay hands on the sick, and they shall recover." At that point he laid aside his church's doctrines about the cessation of miracles and about a God who doesn't heal. He instead dared to believe the Lord's unchanging Word.

He prayed for his wife again. This time he refused to pray the traditional words "if it be Thy will" as he had done each time before. He laid his hands on either side of her head and prayed according to God's Word, and she was miraculously healed of advanced and terminal tuberculosis! (At that time, John G. Lake hadn't yet received the baptism of the Holy Spirit, but God soon remedied that situation.)

When God's call on his life became unmistakable and unavoidable, John G. Lake closed the door to his offices, gave up his successful businesses and launched into a full-time ministry without a divinity degree or an established salary.

He became known as one of the greatest faith healers of the twentieth century, and he ignited one of the greatest missionary movements in South African history. He also established "healing rooms" in Spokane, Washington, where people came from around the world to experience the power of God and be delivered from sickness and oppression.

> ## Healing is not a promise—it is an established fact.

HEALING: THE MINISTRY OF EVERY BELIEVER

God anointed John G. Lake (and many others as well) to redig the ancient well of divine healing. Dr. Lake's words still cut straight to the heart of the American church long after his death in 1935:

> Instead of praying, "Lord, if it be thy will" when you pray for the sick, *lay hands on them just as Jesus commanded.* It is the *ministry of every believer.* And if your ministers and churches do not believe it, God have mercy on them.[2]

This is the problem: Perfect faith cannot exist where the will of God is not known.

This is the will and plan of God: Healing is not a promise—it is an established fact.

How can I make such a claim? It is in God's Word! If God didn't want to heal you, He wouldn't have said that He did. Your Bible says:

> But he was wounded for our transgressions, he was bruised for our iniquities: the chastisement of our peace was upon him; and *with his stripes we are healed.* All we

125

like sheep have gone astray; we have turned every one to his own way; and the LORD hath laid on him the iniquity of us all.

—ISAIAH 53:5–6, EMPHASIS ADDED

Divine healing is so linked with the forgiveness of sins in this passage that they cannot be separated. John G. Lake said, *"It does not take a bit more faith to be healed from your sickness than it does to be saved from your sins."*[3] Healing is not a promise—it is an established fact—just as our salvation is a fact that was established and completed on the cross.

John G. Lake received the revelation that God wants to heal people today just as Jesus willed for healings to take place in New Testament times. But even after John G. Lake, God wanted more digging of divine healing done at that well. He raised up the anointed healing ministry of Aimee Semple McPherson and inspired her to build the five-thousand-seat Angelus Temple in Los Angeles during the 1920s as a bold statement of faith.[4]

During the 1940s, the fiery healing ministries of A. A. Allen, Jack Coe and Oral Roberts exploded over the radio waves from large tent meetings and auditoriums around the nation. People were beginning to believe that God was still in the healing business, even though some "educated" scholars were preaching that God was dead.

More than three decades after Dr. Lake's death, a teenager named Rod Parsley was listening to another voice coming from the well of healing. The sound of Kathryn Kuhlman's slightly odd pronunciation still echoes in my memories as she said, *"I believe in miracles because I believe in God."*[5] She spent most of the time in her services worshiping the Lord, teaching what the Bible says about healing and making it clear that she herself could heal no one—it was Jesus who did the work.

Most of the countless healings in her meetings took place

as she taught on the Holy Spirit. She rarely laid hands on people because she didn't need to—they were healed before they even came to the platform! Blind eyes and deaf ears opened, wheelchairs emptied (they had to be hauled away from her meetings by the truckload at times) and missing limbs grew back!

It is time to redig the well of divine healing *in our day,* friend! Who among us will pay the price to believe God at His Word and step out by faith? Who will dare to command every sickness, every disease, every malady, every pain and every infirmity to bow before the name of Jesus Christ of Nazareth?

Are you ready to say to the sick and oppressed in Jesus' name, "I loose you now by the anointing of the Holy Spirit. Be healed from the top of your head to the soles of your feet"? Remember the words of Dr. Lake: *"It is the ministry of every believer!"*

Drink deeply from the living waters of this ancient well and begin to set people free in Jesus' name. Are you brave enough and bold enough to reach out and take hold of the anointing power of God? If you are, it will revitalize you and those you lay hands on in the name of Jesus!

THE TERRIBLE EFFECTS OF UNBELIEF

Consider the terrible effect that the spiritual cancer called *unbelief* had on the ministry of the Son of God when He went to His own hometown to preach:

> And he could there do no mighty work, save that he laid his hands upon a few sick folk, and healed them. And he marvelled because of their unbelief.
>
> —MARK 6:5–6

It is interesting to me that the Bible describes healing as something considerably less than a "mighty work." Scripture seems to say that healing was what Jesus did when He couldn't really do the "big stuff."

The Bible says Jesus marveled because of the unbelief in His hometown folks. Notice it did not say He marveled at their doubt. Why does the Bible make the distinction? Doubt does not destroy the miracle-working power of God—*unbelief does*. Doubt says, "I *wonder* if it could be." Unbelief declares with confidence, "I *know* it's not."

Jesus responded by going "round about the villages, teaching" (Mark 6:6). It seems that *sound Bible teaching* is God's preferred countermeasure for actions of unbelief. Once you remove unbelief from the picture, healing is elementary!

THREE QUESTIONS TO A MIRACLE

How do you move from a place of unbelief to a place of believing in miracles and healing? *All you have to do is answer three questions.* The answers to those questions lay the foundation for divine healing, miracles, deliverance, prosperity, victory and an abundance of joy, peace, hope or even a happier marriage.

1. Answer the leper's question: "Lord, if thou wilt..." (Mark 1:40).

Just put yourself in that scene. The very first question you must answer as you approach God to receive your healing is this: *Lord, is it Your will to heal me?* Faith can never exist where there is doubt concerning the perfect will of God to heal. Yes, you might get healed through my faith or through the faith of someone else, but you will probably lose it on the way out the door of the church if you don't have your own faith to maintain it.

I used to pray the words "if it be Thy will" for healing before I read and believed God's Word. Since I was a good denominational boy, I would get on my knees and pray, "O God! If it is Your will..."

Do you know what my doubt-filled prayers produced?

Seven members of my immediate family died within eighteen months while I faithfully (or faithlessly) prayed, "If it be Your will…"

I practically grew up in a funeral home listening to preacher after preacher trying to explain how it was God's will that "another flower has been picked for the bouquet of heaven."

I found out later that God had given me an entire Book that declares His will for man and for His kingdom. If you can find it in that Book, it belongs to you, regardless of what erroneous theory other people come up with.

Settle the matter once and for all: *God does not want you to be sick.*

Throughout my studies of the Scriptures, I have found only one person—a leper—who ever asked Jesus if He was willing to heal. All three of the synoptic Gospels record the incident and Jesus' remarkable answer:

> And, behold, there came a leper and worshipped him, saying, Lord, if thou wilt, thou canst make me clean. And Jesus put forth his hand, and touched him, saying, *I will; be thou clean.* And immediately his leprosy was cleansed.
>
> —MATTHEW 8:2–3, EMPHASIS ADDED;
> CF. MARK 1:40–41; LUKE 5:12–13

Settle the matter once and for all: *God does not want you to be sick.* And don't think God caused your sickness because He doesn't have any sickness in His house! God does not have a cancerous tumor carefully reserved for you somewhere in heaven; it would not be able to stand in His presence. God didn't give the cancer to you; the devil did. That means you have no business claiming it "for His glory."

The devil will lie to you, but God's Word is still true. I had an odd growth show up on my side a few years ago, and the first thing the devil said to me was, "Seven members of your immediate family died in eighteen months—and five of them died of cancer. You have cancer. Just look at that tumor on your body!"

Instead of accepting what the devil was saying, I just put a bandage over the growth and focused on God's Word. The devil tried to remind me of my earthly genetic line, but the Bible reminded me that God—my heavenly Father—had sent His Word to heal me, and I reminded the devil of my heavenly genetic line through Jesus!

Every time I accidentally touched that growth, pain would shoot down my side, but I never took off the bandage until it finally came off of its own accord one night in my sleep.

When I awoke the next morning, I noticed the ugly growth lying on the bandage on my bed. Fingerlike tentacles protruded out of the heart of that growth, tentacles that had come right out of my body. But as of that morning there was no sign the tumor ever even existed! Why? Because God is, has always been and always will be a Healer!

There is not one place in the Bible where Jesus ever denied healing to someone who came to Him in faith. You won't find a single place in the Gospels of Matthew, Mark, Luke or John where He refused to perform a miracle! The idea that God won't heal today is just a man-made doctrine thought up by religious people who didn't have any faith.

Faith cannot exist where the will of God is unknown. Beware! The Bible says the traditions of men make God's Word void and "of no effect." (See Matthew 15:6.) Remember, faith cannot exist where there is doubt concerning God's perfect will to heal, save or deliver people today. Healing is not a promise; healing is a fact! God didn't *promise* you anything; He *established* it by His Word.

You may ask, "Lord, is it Your will to heal me?"

Jesus' response will always be, *"I will! Be thou made whole."* (See Mark 1:41.)

2. Answer the doubting father's question: "Can You?"

"And often [the demon] has thrown him both into the fire and into the water to destroy him. *But if You can do anything,* have compassion on us and help us." Jesus said to him, *"If you can believe, all things are possible to him who believes."* Immediately the father of the child cried out and said with tears, "Lord, I believe; help my unbelief!" When Jesus saw that the people came running together, He rebuked the unclean spirit, saying to it, "Deaf and dumb spirit, I command you, come out of him and enter him no more!"

—MARK 9:22–25, NKJV, EMPHASIS ADDED

Today, I believe Jesus would answer the doubting father: "It is not a question of *what I can do,* but rather, it's a question of *what you can believe.* For all things are possible if you can believe."

It is not a question of what God can do for you. It is a question of what you believe He can and will do.

Several years ago I heard the story of a teenager named Betty who was born with her limbs twisted one on top of the other. She had never been able to wear a normal piece of clothing because her body was so grossly deformed. She was unable to eat unless fed through a tube or helped to sip slowly from a straw.

One day Betty's mom said, "Honey, do you know when the Lord is going to heal you?"

Betty asked, "When?" even though she had already been told by Jesus Himself.

Her mom smiled and said, "At three o'clock on Sunday, August 24."

Betty thought that she had told her secret. "Mom, how did you know? Did I let it slip and tell you?"

"No," her mother replied. "The same God that talks to you talks to me."

The Lord had told both of them that He was planning to come into Betty's room and heal her.

Betty asked her mother, "Mom, will you get me a dress and a pair of those shiny patent leather shoes?"

She hadn't had on anything but a nightgown since she became sick. So when Jesus healed her, she wanted to have some clothes to wear to church that night.

Betty's mother told her friends at church, and word began to spread. Everyone began to arrive after service that day. They were about to witness Jesus' miracle-working power.

At three o'clock in the afternoon, a little white cloud appeared in the living room and moved down the hallway into Betty's room. It stopped at the foot of Betty's bed, and she began to struggle to reach for it. She couldn't reach very far with her twisted limbs, and finally she fell over in exhaustion.

Jesus then told her, "Betty, I am giving you the desire of your heart to be healed. You are normal and well. You have health now. You are completely well because I healed you."

After a short pause, He continued, "Now, remember, every day look at the clouds and watch. The next time you see Me coming in a cloud, I will not leave you here. I will take you to be with Me forever."

The cloud moved over the bed, and eyewitnesses said the room was filled with sounds as if someone were cracking tree limbs. It was actually the sound of Betty's twisted bones as they moved back into place. After spending fifteen years as a hopeless invalid, Betty rose up out of her bed.

She put on the dress her mother had bought for her, and it hung on her body like a flour sack. Her shoes didn't fit either, but that didn't stop her from running all around the house.[6] Not only *will* God heal, but *He can!*

3. Answer God's question to you: "Will you?"

Now there is at Jerusalem by the sheep market a pool, which is called in the Hebrew tongue Bethesda, having five porches. In these lay a great multitude of impotent folk, of blind, halt, withered, waiting for the moving of the water. For an angel went down at a certain season into the pool, and troubled the water: whosoever then first after the troubling of the water stepped in was made whole of whatsoever disease he had. And a certain man was there, which had an infirmity thirty and eight years. When Jesus saw him lie, and knew that he had been now a long time in that case, he saith unto him, *Wilt thou be made whole?*

—JOHN 5:2–6, EMPHASIS ADDED

WILL YOU?

First we must answer the question, "Will God?" and then the question, "Can God?" But the third question is not asked of God, but rather asked by God of you: *Will you?*

The man by the pool had lain there for thirty-eight years, waiting to be healed. Jesus confronted this man's doubt and asked him, "Do you want to be made whole?" The man did exactly what so many of us do when God asks us if we want to be whole—he *immediately came up with an excuse.* Technically, the man's answer was correct. Spiritually, however, it was a way of sidestepping Jesus' question.

What was the man's answer? He said to Jesus:

> *Sir, I have no man,* when the water is troubled, to put me into the pool: but *while I am coming, another steppeth down before me.* Jesus saith unto him, *Rise, take up thy bed, and walk.* And immediately the *man* was made whole, and took up his bed, and walked: and on the same day was the sabbath.
>
> —JOHN 5:7–9, EMPHASIS ADDED

The man had no ability to do what Jesus had asked him to do until he dared to take a step of faith *before* he was made whole. Jesus told him to take up his bed and walk. As soon as he forgot about his "needing a man" to help—as soon as he let go of the emotional pain of losing out on healing for all those years—supernatural strength flooded his limbs, and long-atrophied muscles exploded with power he had never experienced before.

This man didn't simply rise from his bed of affliction—*he carried it off like a victor carrying the spoils of battle!* That beggar's mat became a trophy of God's power in his life—and he never even touched the healing waters of the pool! "Your *faith* has made you whole."

I have heard Norvel Hayes, a great teacher of the Word of God and personal friend, tell a wonderful story of God's healing power many times in his meetings. He was preparing for a meeting one day when the enemy attacked his physical body. The devil tried to convince him it was pneumonia as he was seized with fits of coughing. His chest felt so tight that he could barely breathe. But the Lord intervened and told him that this was not *his* affliction.

The enemy hoped to stop Brother Norvel from going to his meeting because God desired to do a great miracle there. God gave him a word of knowledge, "There will be a blind man there, and I will open his eyes."

Brother Norvel went on to the meeting and was told that a multimillionaire businessman who had been a great blessing to the kingdom of God would be there that night. The Lord told Brother Norvel, "When you get there, all I want you to do is tell the story of blind Bartimaeus, and I'll open that man's eyes."

After the meeting started, somebody introduced the businessman and invited him to the pulpit to give his testimony. Brother Norvel could see the man out of the corner of his eye, and then he heard a tapping sound. The blind businessman was making his way down the aisle toward the pulpit, tapping ahead of himself with a white cane. He reached the front of the church, gave his testimony and then returned to his seat in the same way.

Brother Norvel rose and immediately shared the story of blind Bartimaeus who had cried out for Jesus even though everyone around him was telling him to be quiet—including Jesus' disciples! But the more people protested, the more the man cried out for the Lord. (See Mark 10:46–52.)

BLIND BARTIMAEUS CRIED OUT—BUT THIS BLIND MAN WOULD NOT

Brother Norvel walked over to the businessman and stood directly in front of him. He said again, "Blind Bartimaeus cried out! He cried out to God! And when he cried out and would not be silenced, God opened his eyes! The blind man cried out!"

Brother Norvel said the man never moved or whispered throughout the whole service. It was one of the most disappointing things he had ever seen. When he returned to his hotel room, the Lord told him, "I've been trying to heal that man for years, but I can't get him to do what I say."

How many times has the Lord given us what seemed to be simple instructions, but they were necessary for us to follow in order to receive our healing? Recall the story of Naaman the leper. The Bible states that he was the captain of the host of Syria, but even though he was a great man, he had contracted leprosy. Gehazi, the servant of the prophet Elisha, was sent to Naaman in order to heal him. The command from the servant was simple and direct: "Dip in the Jordan River seven times." (See 2 Kings 5:10.)

Unfortunately, pride overcame Naaman. He became angry that Elisha had not come to minister personally to him. Didn't Elisha understand how powerful Naaman was?

Naaman's servants questioned him, saying, "If the prophet had asked you to do some great or difficult thing, wouldn't you have done it?" Recognizing the error of his ways, Naaman *obeyed the Word of the Lord through the man who was sent, and he received his healing.* (See 2 Kings 5:11–14.)

THE ARM OF THE LORD
STRETCHES FORTH TO HEAL

Isaiah 53:1 proclaims, "Who hath believed our report? and to whom is the arm of the LORD revealed?"

Allow me to answer Isaiah 53:1 in this way: The arm of the Lord is revealed to that man or woman who believes His report!

What does the arm of the Lord represent? It represents redemption, healing and deliverance. With His fingers, He flung the planets and stars into existence. By His strong hands, God created the world. However, it took His entire arm to rescue lost and dying humanity from Satan's grip.

The prophet Isaiah goes on to say of the coming Redeemer, "Surely he hath borne our griefs, and carried our sorrows: yet we did esteem him stricken, smitten of God, and afflicted. But he was wounded for our transgressions, he was bruised for our iniquities: the chastisement of our peace was upon him; and with his stripes we are healed" (Isa. 53:4–5).

Our Lord and Savior, Jesus Christ, took upon Himself the sins of the world—our sins.

The arm of the Lord is revealed to that man or woman who believes His report!

The very tendency of mankind to sin was laid upon Him. Jesus, the Anointed One who destroys every yoke, became burdened with our iniquities. He paid the ultimate price for our salvation, which includes the healing of our bodies.

We have all experienced heartaches and disappointment throughout life. I'm not talking to you about something I haven't been through myself. I know what it is like to wake up every day of my life and struggle against sickness and disease in my own family. Seven members of my immediate family have died within a short period of time.

Did you ever praise God when it took every ounce of your strength to get just one "hallelujah" out of your lips? Did you ever lift up your hands in worship even when the feelings just weren't there? Have you ever said, "Praise the Lord," when what you really wanted to do was sit silently in discouragement and seeming defeat? Yet, it is in the chief Cornerstone, Jesus Christ, that we receive our strength.

HEALING IS A FACT, NOT JUST A PROMISE

Do you know what it feels like to have the enemy jeering at you while you preach the healing of the Lord? But even as I declare God's healing power, I am able to stand in faith.

Soon after the tragedy that struck my family, I discovered that it is God's will to heal. I then began to witness the miraculous take place. I watched God's healing power at work in my mother who had a massive heart attack at the age of twenty-nine. I saw my sister, Debbie, delivered from several prescription drugs she began taking as a result of a car accident many years ago.

Healing is a fact, not just a mere promise. That is why God's question to you is, *"Will you be made whole?"* Will you take a real step of faith? It is easy to hear about Jesus' healing blood, but the real test comes when you are faced with a situation in your own life or family that only the Great Physician can touch. When you take a step of faith to stand upon His Word, your trial can become your testimony. Regardless of what the doctors may say, they can be proven wrong on every count because there is a God in heaven who still heals!

God has worked miracle after miracle of healing in my family. But it has taken persistent belief in, and obedience to, His holy Word.

The same can happen in your life. When you plant the seed of obedience into the soil of impossibility, you will reap a great harvest! It is time to redig the ancient well of divine healing. God has not changed, nor has His arm grown weak.

We serve the God of love who raises people from the dead, heals blind eyes, opens deaf ears, stops the flow of fatal hemorrhages, destroys cancer, reverses the HIV/AIDS virus and

When you plant the seed of obedience into the soil of impossibility, you will reap a great harvest!

stops every other disease in its tracks. Redig the well of healing and drink deeply of the rejuvenation of the Lord!

Collision of the Kingdoms

Chapter **9**

*And these signs shall follow them that believe;
In my name shall they cast out devils.*
—MARK 16:17

Our world is a dangerous place in which to live these days. It is filled with wars and rumors of wars. Children are killing children. The blood of innocents has flowed in New York, Washington, D.C. and the Middle East. Good is called evil, and evil is trumpeted as good.

I have news for you: The door of damnation has been opened, and satanic hordes have been released over the earth. There's a devil loose in our world!

The good news is that Jesus Christ defeated Satan on a rugged cross more than two thousand years ago. He then gave us the power to keep the devil in his place.

The church of the first century barely broke its stride to deal with demonic manifestations in a service or even in a public market. It was nothing for church leaders to counter and publicly embarrass professional sorcerers they encountered in their ministries. (See Acts 13:6–11.)

If demons dared to interrupt the preaching of the gospel, the early church leaders *commanded* the unclean spirits, "Come out! Do it *now* in Jesus' name!" The demand was nonnegotiable, and there is no biblical record of lengthy interviews, compilations of family histories and checklists or extensive counseling. A demon was a demon, and a believer was just that—*a believer.*[1]

It seems the early church understood that there is only one thing to be done with a demon—it is to be cast out in Jesus' name! The early church had no interest in conducting long conversations with the demons; they just wanted to be rid of them and to free the afflicted person.

DEMONS ARE BASKING IN OUR CHURCH PEWS

What about the church today? Most American churches would have a problem even recognizing demonic manifestations. Many would be more prone to call a psychiatrist to deal with the situation than to call on the name of Jesus. If a demonic manifestation did occur and they managed to recognize it as such, most churches and ministers wouldn't know the first thing to do about it!

Demons are basking in an atmosphere of Satan's liking, and they aren't about to change it. They can put up with a little Bible reading as long as no one believes it; hymns sung with the fervor of a funeral dirge become lullabies to the demonic spirits lurking in the back of the sanctuaries.

It is time to redig another ancient well of our fathers, a well that traces directly back to the ministry of Jesus Christ Himself. The well of deliverance from demonic power was filled in and covered by the debris of spiritual apostasy and unbelief during the Dark Ages, and few people remembered it even existed.

God called a man to redig this well in his own life under the guidance of spiritual pioneers such as Dr. Howard Carter and Smith Wigglesworth. This man was my mentor and spiritual father, the late Dr. Lester Sumrall.

THE TRUE PURPOSE OF SUPERNATURAL POWER

Dr. Sumrall redug the well of deliverance in the bedrock of the mission field. He ministered in more than a hundred nations, where few, if any, restraints existed to curtail the advance of evil.

It was in the heat of battle and the urgency of the spiritual front line that God taught Dr. Sumrall the true purpose of supernatural power in the believer. That purpose is to deliver those in bondage and work *signs and wonders* before the lost that will lead them to a saving knowledge of Jesus Christ.

One of Dr. Sumrall's greatest adventures in divine deliverance involved Clarita Villanueva, a young girl who was being bitten by devils. She was an inmate at Biblibid Prison, an infamous prison in Manila, the capital city of the Philippines.[2]

Radio stations and newspapers spread the news throughout the island nation that this young girl was experiencing strange bite marks, which would appear on her body from no known source. Scientists from all over the world came to study the phenomena and attempt to discover the cause of the bites, but they were without success. It was in this mix of heightened public interest that God spoke directly to Dr. Sumrall to go to the prison and set her free.

Dr. Sumrall learned that the demons made Clarita act like an animal one moment and like a sorceress the next. One day while being questioned in the office of the Chief of Police, she had fallen to the floor and crawled under the desk.

The chief kicked her and said, "Come out from under there!"

She crawled out and began to whine, "I've lost my cross."

He told her he didn't know anything about her cross. He even turned his pockets inside out, saying, "You see, I don't have it."

She looked at him with a strange look and then said, "Look again."

Disgusted, he plunged his hand back into his pocket. There was her small cross! Chills ran down his spine. Less than thirty seconds after he had thrust his hands into his empty pockets, even turning them wrong-side out, the cross mysteriously appeared there![3]

"THE DEVIL IS DEAD!"

Dr. Sumrall had a word from the Lord, but he still had to put feet to his faith. He explains in his book, *101 Questions & Answers on Demon Powers:*

> I went to see the mayor of Manila and also the head doctor of Bilibid Prison to get permission to pray for her, then set a subsequent date to return and pray for her. I felt that I needed time in fasting and prayer before ministering to her. It became evident that the spirit would not have moved had I not spent this time in prayer before God with fasting.[4]

Once inside the prison, Dr. Sumrall prayed for the girl for many hours over a span of several days. Finally he placed his hands on each side of her head and cried out, "Come out of her, you evil and wicked spirit of hell! Come out of her in the name of Jesus," and she experienced a mighty deliverance.

God wants us to confront the demons of darkness wherever we find them and cast them out in His name as a sign to the unbelievers around us.

On one occasion when the demons tried to return, Clarita screamed for God to deliver her in the name of Jesus.[5] When she did this, she grabbed for something in what appeared to be thin air and then fainted. The doctors later found strands of long, black, coarse hair in her hand. Research conducted on the hair samples revealed that the strands of hair were not from any living creature on earth.

The story of her deliverance was so great that it made the headlines, *and over five hundred thousand were saved*. One newspaper article even read, "The Devil Is Dead."[6]

God wants to re-create these kinds of "Elijah encounters" in the lives of believers today. He wants us to confront the demons of darkness wherever we find them and cast them out in His name as a sign to the unbelievers around us.

Well, that sounds pretty radical, Pastor Parsley, you may be thinking. It does, doesn't it? I wish I had thought of it myself, but I didn't—Jesus did:

> And these *signs* shall follow *them that believe;* in my name shall they *cast out devils*...
> —MARK 16:17, EMPHASIS ADDED

Jesus also said:

> Behold, *I give unto you power* to tread on serpents and scorpions, and *over all the power of the enemy:* and nothing shall by any means hurt you.
> —LUKE 10:19, EMPHASIS ADDED

God has called us to rise above the status quo of so-called church normalcy to impose the authority of a holy God on the hidden, unholy forces impacting our society. We've lived too long in a culture where right has been framed as wrong, and righteousness has been seen as something strange or abnormal. That is the direct result of the dark forces that surround us, demonic influences that the church is called to cast out in the name of Jesus!

THE CHURCH HASN'T GONE FAR ENOUGH!

The devil has gone too far, and the church hasn't gone far enough! We think we can waltz in, wave a magic wand and deliver people from Satan's power even though we don't pay the price of living holy lives. We must diligently study God's Word and spend enough time in prayer to know the Father's heart.

Dr. Sumrall personally believed that fasting and prayer were important preparations for deliverance. He fasted and prayed before virtually every planned encounter in his ministry. For example, he described the time he prayed for the daughter of Go Puan Seng, a Chinese friend who owned a newspaper in Manila.

> He asked me to pray for his daughter who was suffering from an evil spirit. I told him that I would fast and pray for two days before going to his house. When we prayed for God to set her free, she was immediately released from the devil's power. In my own experience I have found it imperative to fast and pray before seeking to set a person free from demon power.[7]

DEMONIC POWER IS RUNNING RAMPANT IN OUR SOCIETY AND IN OUR WORLD

We don't want to believe it, but over a period of time the doctrine of some "religious" leaders has slowly and steadily eroded the well of deliverance to the point that it is nearly useless and beyond recognition. Their views and opinions have permeated the mind-set of many in the body of Christ to the point that we now call good "evil," and evil "good."

We go to church on Sunday, vote pro choice on Monday (endorsing the wholesale murder of innocent, unborn children), call the psychic fortuneteller from the television informercial on Tuesday and play in the church poker

146

fundraiser on Wednesday night.

We are more materially prosperous than at any other time in history, but we are teetering on the edge of moral bankruptcy. We have discovered the cure for many diseases, yet we still kill our unborn and allow physician-assisted suicide in some states. We even condone lying and cheating as long as it doesn't hurt anyone.

Demonic power is running rampant in our society and the world. Ancient demon spirits have been dispatched throughout the United States as messengers of vengeance, operating through living human beings. They wreak havoc—killing, stealing and destroying whatever and whomever they can.

Social, economic and political reforms are good, but the power of God in demonstration is better.

The list of demonic "vessels" is long, and they range from a mother who drowns her own children to the Muslim terrorists who struck America on September 11, 2001 and instantly killed thousands.

International madmen perpetrate perverted schemes of violence while politicians negotiate away our religious freedoms, enact legislation to protect the lewd and underwrite the indecent. Meanwhile, the hidden and dangerous devotees of hardcore Satanism continue to grow, enticing into their lair everyone from doctors to lawyers, politicians to housewives and even some misguided preachers.

THE ONSLAUGHT OF EVIL IS NOT OF HUMAN ORIGIN

All this onslaught of evil is too subtle and too sinister to be of human origin. It is the carefully calculated conspiracy of demonic spirits. Is there cause to fear? Is all hope lost? Hardly!

The apostle Paul warned Timothy nearly two thousand years ago:

> Now the Spirit speaketh expressly, that in the latter times some shall depart from the faith, giving heed to seducing spirits, and doctrines of devils; speaking lies in hypocrisy; having their conscience seared with a hot iron.
>
> —1 TIMOTHY 4:1–2

Even in the wake of the greatest foreign attack on American soil in modern history, rebellion against God's authority is still at an all-time high. After all, the hold-over motto of the day is, "If it feels good, do it!"

That's what the people in Noah's time thought. They went on eating, drinking and making merry until the day came that the door was shut upon the ark. Jesus prophesied that in the latter days it would be the same. He warned:

> But as the days of Noe were, so shall also the coming of the Son of man be. For as in the days that were before the flood they were eating and drinking, marrying and giving in marriage, until the day that Noe entered into the ark, and knew not until the flood came, and took them all away; so shall also the coming of the Son of man be.
>
> —MATTHEW 24:37–39

THERE'S A DEVIL ON THE LOOSE!

The demonic has even tainted the ministry of the gospel. Someone once asked me to preach at a meeting attended by a large number of pastors and ministers from many different denominations. When it was time for me to minister, I felt prompted to say, "I can tell you what your problem is: There's a devil loose!"

Many of the ministers in attendance that day were sporting their finest religious trappings, and many of them were even wearing priestly vestments or the robes of bishops. There's nothing wrong with that if it appeals to you, but make sure there is purity and holiness in the heart beating under those priestly garments.

The host had asked me to come and teach at the meeting, but I had heard from the Lord, and He had other plans. I said, "What I'm about to do is see you delivered from reading and watching pornography when you think no one is looking. God wants to deliver you from a lustful and adulterous spirit."

I continued, "We have some ministers here who need to throw their *Playboy* magazines away. Every man in this believer's meeting who needs deliverance from homosexuality, sexual perversion or incest—stand up right now!"

The host preacher nearly swallowed his tongue when three-fourths of the audience stood up—including two-thirds of the people on *the platform.*

When these sorts of things are coming to pass, you must know that spiritual wickedness in heavenly places has been loosed in the land. Yet, I have good news for you...

There is still a God who creates. There is still a King who redeems. There is still a Lamb who bears the marks of His sacrifice. There is still a victorious, triumphant church of Jesus Christ against which the gates of hell shall not prevail! (See Matthew 16:18.)

My friend, social, economic and political reforms are good, but the power of God in demonstration is better. Directly after the 9-11 attack on America, there was a resurgence in faith and a renewed focus on the things of God, but that change toward faith in Jesus Christ has begun to diminish.

Consider that pollster Andrew Kohut said, "I've never seen such a dramatic change disappear so quickly," referring to the rapid rise and then subsequent decrease of the effects of religion in America.[8]

Part of the problem is our timid spirit and weak knees. We

promote the dead letter of the law and minimize the power of the Holy Spirit to change and deliver people. When a wife-beater comes to your altar, when people come to you saying they are tormented at night or battle with alcoholism, perversion, promiscuity or homosexuality, they don't need counseling. They need a long, cold, drink from the ancient well of deliverance!

It's time to redig the ancient well of our fathers—the well of deliverance from demonic power. More and more we will find ourselves ministering the gospel of Jesus Christ to people bound in demonic bondages of sexual perversion such as homosexuality and lesbianism. Alcoholism and substance abuse abound in societies ruled by pleasure and the adoration of self. We must be prepared to set the captives free in the hour of decision.

DELIVERANCE: WHAT HAPPENS WHEN TWO KINGDOMS COLLIDE

In my book *On the Brink,* I described what happens when the kingdom of God collides with the kingdom of darkness:

> By the terms *kingdom of heaven* and *kingdom of God,* we refer to "anywhere the rule of God is *imposed.*" Notice that I did not say it is where the rule of God is "enforced." There is a world of difference between enforcement and imposition. God's kingdom is destined to be imposed where it is not welcome.
>
> You enforce a thing by requiring obedience to a set of standards, limitations or requirements *agreed upon* by a society or government. Our authority goes far beyond enforcement and into the realm of imposition. We have a mandate to *impose* the rule of God over every spirit in existence and, where necessary, over every human being influenced by rebellious spirits.[9]

It is time for us to redig the well of deliverance from demonic powers and to distribute its life-giving waters to everyone around us. Many who are bound and oppressed by the devil cannot help themselves—but *you* have the power to help them. *Impose* the power of the kingdom of God upon the powers of darkness that bind them. Then, ask them if they want to receive Jesus Christ as their Lord and Savior.

If all of this sounds new or foreign to you, begin with an examination of your own life. Wherever you are right now, freedom is only seconds away! If you sensed while reading this chapter that demonic oppression plagues you, then lay your hand on your heart and pray this prayer of deliverance:

> *Whether I am tormented by demon power or strug-*
> *gling under the weight of curses or occult activity, in*
> *the name of Jesus, I command that spirit to come out!*
> *I command that oppression of darkness to lift and go*
> *in Jesus' name!*

I declare that every accusing spirit is cast down in your life right now. They have lost their hold on your life. Walk free, child of God, in Jesus' name!

"One Like Me"

Chapter 10

But ye shall receive power, after that the Holy
Ghost is come upon you: and ye shall be
witnesses unto me...
—Acts 1:8

T he nation was known for its music and entertainment, for its independent spirit and its rich sports heritage, but something was terribly wrong. The bars flourished while the powerless and passionless churches dried up. Gambling and greed were beginning to dominate virtually every activity and captivate the nation's middle class.

As the hunger for personal pleasure began to dominate the culture, prostitution began to invade the nation's streets. Murder, rape and other violent crimes increased so quickly that there were not enough police officers in the entire country to restore order or to even slow down the crime spree.[1]

Then a former coal miner, a believer who would carry his beloved Bible into the mines with him, began to cry out to heaven during a thirteen-month period of intense prayer and intercession for revival in the land.

The revival he so desperately sought was birthed in that young man's heart as the Holy Spirit began to awaken Evan Roberts each morning at 1:00 A.M. for four hours of intimate communion with God. The Spirit would come again at 9:00 A.M. and take him into a "great expanse" for another four-hour period of communion in the Spirit. This went on for about three months, and eventually Roberts' landlady threw him out because he became so "enthusiastic" in his prayers in his room that she began to fear him![2]

Roberts didn't realize it at that time, but God was crafting a spiritual bomb in that room. He unleashed fiery Evan Roberts on Wales in 1904 along with a small ministry team. This young preacher, who delivered an unusual message of "praying in the Spirit," had a vision in which one hundred thousand souls would come to Christ. His vision came to pass through what would quickly be called *the Welsh Revival*.

Six weeks into the revival, as many as twenty thousand people had come to the Lord, and newspaper accounts spread the news around the world. Revival began to break out in other countries as people read the accounts of what was happening in Wales. Many of the greatest preachers and Christian leaders of the times, including Rees Howells and G. Campbell Morgan, came to witness it. It was called the "Pentecost greater than Pentecost." The impact this fiery revival made in America, India, Africa, Europe and Great Britain still qualifies it as the greatest revival in history.

Evan Roberts was one of the early pioneers who redug the well of the Holy Spirit and released God's power like a fire in the dry timber of human hearts.

Jesus' Power Remains on the Earth
Through the Holy Spirit

The real fire was ignited thousands of years before Evan Roberts came on the scene; it was lit the moment the One called Immanuel—God with us—invaded the earth encased in the flesh and blood of a tiny baby and changed the course of human history forever. Jehovah's Son

God openly and unapologetically gave us the supernatural baptism of the Holy Spirit in power to continue the supernatural work of Christ in the earth.

became a man and lived among us. His mission was to turn the direction of the human race away from hell and toward the God of heaven.

When Jesus Christ ascended on high once again, He made provision for His supernatural presence to remain in the earth. He made a way for His healing power, His delivering power, His prophetic power and His declarative and creative power to remain in the earth in an even greater measure!

Many Christians are fond of quoting the following Scripture passage, and I include myself in that number:

> Verily, verily, I say unto you, He that believeth on me, the works that I do shall he do also; and greater works than these shall he do; because I go unto my Father.
> —John 14:12

The only problem I see is that we don't put enough emphasis on the *agency* of that promise, described by Jesus in the next four verses:

> And whatsoever ye shall ask in my name, that will I do, that the Father may be glorified in the Son. If ye shall ask any thing in my name, I will do it. If ye love me, keep my

commandments. And I will pray the Father, and he shall give you another Comforter, that he may abide with you for ever.

—JOHN 14:13–16, EMPHASIS ADDED

I don't know about you, but I'd love to be part of a church that *does even greater works than Jesus did in His lifetime!* We know this isn't happening the way it should—especially in the United States. But how could it change? When we *yield to Him.* He can do more and greater works because He has the opportunity to multiply the distribution of His miracle-working power through millions of hands instead of just His own.

SPIRITUAL PARAPLEGIA: SEVERED FROM THE POWER SOURCE

Unfortunately, it appears we have somehow become severed from the power source, our Head, Jesus Christ. By all outward signs, a form of spiritual paraplegia has set in, bringing all movement, progress and outward activity to a disappointing halt in many churches. We need to reset the master switch!

Perhaps too many members of the body of Christ have discounted the very One Jesus sent to help make it happen. By discounting, explaining away or openly scoffing at the supernatural work of the Holy Spirit, they disqualify themselves for the true enduement from on high described in Luke 24:49. God openly and unapologetically gave us the supernatural baptism of the Holy Spirit in power to continue the supernatural work of Christ in the earth.

God is obviously supernatural. The new birth in Christ is supernatural. So why isn't the church demonstrating supernatural power the way Jesus did? He said we are supposed to. Why don't we walk and minister in power the way the disciples did after their Pentecostal baptism in fire? The churches and believers of the first century made such an impact on their societies that they literally transformed entire nations, cultures and world empires. Our churches often don't have enough power to transform the sinners in their own pews, let alone reach their cities or nations through the anointing of the Holy Spirit. Why?

Undervalued, Overlooked and Greatly Reduced

I'm convinced that at least one reason is because we have undervalued, overlooked and greatly reduced the role of the Holy Spirit in the church of today. Let me repeat a modified version of something I said earlier: *We don't perform the miracles they did because we won't make the sacrifices they did.*

The modern critics of those who believe in the infilling power of the Holy Spirit claim that God only worked miracles and moved supernaturally through the apostles during the first century. According to this theory called *cessationism,* the supernatural work of the Holy Spirit (apart from the work of regeneration at salvation) ceased to exist with the passing of the original apostles.

Check your Bible, and I'm positive you will find it reads exactly as mine does. I've noticed that the Book of Acts and the Epistles are filled with the names of men and women who don't have recognized apostolic status. The Holy Spirit was given to *everyone,* not just to the twelve apostles of Jesus Christ.

The Holy Spirit is not some third-string, watered-down, four-times-removed-by-marriage, second cousin of God. *He is God,* and His power is unlimited, unfathomable, immeasurable and altogether holy.

His ministry did not somehow cease to exist or get packed away in storage when the original twelve apostles died. Paul demonstrated the power of the Holy Spirit, and he wasn't an "apostle of the Lamb." Others operated in supernatural gifts that can be attributed only to the Holy Spirit, and they were not clergy as we see them in the modern sense.

HOW MANY STARS DO YOU SEE?

Have you ever noticed Luke's detailed description of the powerhouse lineup at the church of Antioch? How many "stars" do you see listed, and what is their status in this particular gathering?

> Now there were in the church that was at Antioch *certain prophets and teachers; as Barnabas, and Simeon that was called Niger, and Lucius of Cyrene, and Manaen,* which had been brought up with Herod the tetrarch, and Saul. As they ministered to the Lord, and fasted, *the Holy Ghost said,* Separate me Barnabas and Saul for the work whereunto I have called them. And *when they had fasted and prayed, and laid their hands on them,* they sent them away.
> —ACTS 13:1–3, EMPHASIS ADDED

Saul (later called Paul) is the only full-fledged "star" who is included in the critic's list of apostles. Barnabas is sometimes grudgingly acknowledged to be a key player, but he is rarely considered an "apostle."

THE HOLY SPIRIT USED PEOPLE WITHOUT REPUTATIONS

One problem is that Barnabas was set apart by the Holy Spirit as a "sent one" (the Greek term is *apostolos,* meaning apostle), along with Saul. The interesting point of this passage is that the people without reputations as apostles somehow managed to hear the voice of the Holy Spirit. They were authorized to lay hands on Barnabas and Saul and send them out as apostles. That speaks of apostolic authority totally separate from the original twelve who were based out of Jerusalem.

It gets even more interesting. According to Acts 21:8–10, Philip the evangelist (another powerhouse without star status) had "four daughters, virgins, which did prophesy" (v. 9). According to the critics, New Testament prophecy allegedly died out with the apostles. They have real problems acknowledging that God would speak through "nonapostolic types"—especially young unmarried women. Yet there it is, written in the Bible.

To make matters worse, another character showed up at Philip's home who also operated as a prophet; his name was Agabus. The list of those who were not apostles but were operating in supernatural gifts just keeps adding up in the Book of Acts!

None of this makes much sense if you see the Holy Spirit as a powerless, mute, secondhand clone sent to be a hall monitor for the church after Jesus had returned to heaven.

The Azusa Street Revival Begins

God used an unknown, one-eyed, African American preacher named William Seymour to totally upend the starched and stuffy American church scene two years after the Welsh Revival burned a path of glory around the world.

Seymour had heard about the supernatural gift of "speaking in other tongues," but he had never found anyone who had actually experienced it. That is, until he met a lady who had received the gift in a church meeting in Houston, Texas. She pointed him north to Topeka and to her former employer, Charles Fox Parham, a white preacher who ran Bethel College, a Holiness Bible School. Seymour soon talked Reverend Parham into allowing him to listen to lectures.

When a lady preacher invited Seymour to speak at her church in Los Angeles, he agreed and then borrowed train fare from Parham for the trip. After the first meeting,

Seymour returned to find himself locked out of the church building due to differences of doctrine. But he remained undaunted. He moved the meeting down the road to a home on Bonnie Brae Avenue.

The Holy Spirit fell on Seymour and several of the people in attendance on the night of April 9, 1906, and history was made. News of the outpouring of the baptism of the Holy Spirit spread quickly, and the meetings were moved to an abandoned church building at 312 Azusa Street.[3]

Four days later, an earthquake nearly destroyed San Francisco, and sinners hungry for God began to flock to the meetings. Attendance at the services began to explode. News reports of the meetings drew people from around the world, including John G. Lake, who would take the fires of the Holy Spirit baptism to Africa. Many major Pentecostal movements were birthed from that small beginning at Azusa Street.

THE PROBLEM WITH THE HOLY SPIRIT IS THAT HE IS SO "SUPERNATURAL"

The greatest difficulty for some who would discount the Holy Spirit is the number of Old and New Testament passages dealing with His work, mission, character and power in the latter days. In other words, the problem with the Holy Spirit is that He is so *supernatural*. All of the biblical references to Him refer to an overtly supernatural work of the Spirit, which is to continue until the completion of God's purposes in the earth. (See John 15:16; John 20:21–22; Acts 1:8.)

My friend, it is time to redig this invaluable and vital well of our fathers called the Holy Spirit! The power of the baptism of the Holy Spirit was so crucial to New Testament Christianity that the apostle Paul asked new converts if they had received it *after* they believed on Christ:

> Paul having passed through the upper coasts came to Ephesus: and finding certain disciples, he said unto them,

Have ye received the Holy Ghost since ye believed? And they said unto him, We have not so much as heard whether there be any Holy Ghost.

—ACTS 19:1–2, EMPHASIS ADDED

Now, that conversation sounds strangely familiar to me. I'm constantly amazed by the number of people who are totally unaware of the nature, ministry and role of God the Holy Spirit.

That is not the case at our church—God the Holy Spirit has already shown up and proven His power to us! The arguments of those who smugly assure us that the days of miracles and supernatural gifts are over mean little to us. **The Holy Spirit of God is the divine delivery system, God's own hand extended to man in the earthly realm.** In our monthly Sunday evening "Miracle, Healing and Victory Service," we often see people healed and delivered at the same time they get gloriously baptized in the Holy Spirit! That is the power of God revealed on earth. It cannot be orchestrated on such a large scale. The greatest of all proofs for these events are the hundreds and thousands of *permanently changed lives.*

You don't get those kinds of miracles when you compromise the Word of God. Christians who insist on explaining away the validity of God's promises limit themselves to receiving only a portion of His reward.

The Holy Spirit of God is the divine delivery system, God's own hand extended to man in the earthly realm. He transfers the riches and unlimited resources of heaven to His vessels on earth. He does this not so we can selfishly have everything that we want, but so that you and I can be witnesses to the life-changing power of our supernatural Lord and Savior, Jesus Christ. Never underestimate the power of the Holy

Spirit! (And never presume to take scissors or an editor's pen to God's Word. See Revelation 22:18–19.)

Do you understand how greatly the Lord wants to work through you in supernatural ways? We waste an incredible amount of time begging God to "do something through us." That prayer has already been answered on the cross. He is waiting for us to adjust our sails to the wind of the Holy Spirit and be transported into the center of His purpose.

Listen to the promise of God spoken thousands of years ago by the prophet Joel:

> Be glad then, ye children of Zion, and rejoice in the Lord your God: for he hath given you the former rain moderately, and he will cause to come down for you the rain, the *former rain, and the latter rain* in the first month. And the floors shall be full of wheat, and the vats shall overflow with wine and oil.
>
> —JOEL 2:23–24, EMPHASIS ADDED

When we look at this passage more closely, a deeper meaning can be gleaned. Wheat is a persistent prophetic symbol for God's Word; oil represents His holy anointing; and wine represents joy or the Holy Spirit. God the Son prayed, God the Father answered and God the Holy Spirit came to dwell with and in us.

If the church is a representation of His body, the body should represent Him. Joel painted a broad picture of the variety present in God's kingdom when he described the kind of people who would respond to the outpouring of the Holy Spirit:

> I will pour out my spirit upon *all flesh;* and your *sons* and your *daughters* shall prophesy, your *old men* shall dream dreams, your *young men* shall see visions: And also upon the *servants* and upon the *handmaids* in those days will I pour out my spirit.
>
> —JOEL 2:28–29, EMPHASIS ADDED

If you are part of that "all flesh" (in other words, if you are a human being) and if you have said *yes* to God's fiery baptism in the Spirit, then Someone holy dwells in you—Someone who is the Anointing. He never sleeps or grows weary. He is God, the Holy Spirit or, in the Hebrew, *ruach ha kodesh* ("the Holy Breath").

His very presence brings divine revelation, strength, comfort and power. Yield to Him so His strength can be made manifest in your weakness (2 Cor. 12:9).

WE SEND FLOWERS TO THE SICK AND DYING INSTEAD OF PRAYING FOR THEM

God commissioned all of us to "do the works of the ministry," to preach the gospel and make disciples of all men. Instead, we preach a form of godliness and deny its power. He anointed us to lay hands on the sick and see them recover, but instead we elect committees to send flowers to the sick and dying rather than praying for them.

We have to do this because many of us preach (or at least secretly believe) that God doesn't heal anymore. We're convinced that if He does heal, then He does it for a privileged few, for reasons we cannot understand. The rest are left to "glorify God" with their sicknesses, diseases and pain. Meanwhile, our committees for honoring sickness and death split the church as they fight over whether to send pansies or petunias.

Once we deny the power of our supernatural God, things can only go from bad to worse. God wasn't caught off guard by our humanity or by our doubt and unbelief. He said, "I'm going to send the former and the latter rain altogether in one month. I will restore everything." (See Joel 2:23.)

What does that mean? That means that apostolic authority is coming back to the church. The church is again receiving the power to deliver the demonized and unleash revival on an unprecedented scale. What kind of scale am I talking about?

The Bible says God intends to cover the earth with His glory.

The first time God covered the earth, He flooded it with water unleashed *from above and beneath*. According to Genesis 7:11, it took a flood from two directions to cover the earth and release God's judgment on the earth: "...the same day were all the fountains of the great deep broken up, and the windows of heaven were opened."

God said, "But truly, as I live, all the earth shall be filled with the glory of the LORD" (Num. 14:21). The prophet Habakkuk linked the first flood with this second flood when he prophesied, "For the earth shall be filled with the knowledge of the glory of the LORD, as the waters cover the sea" (Hab. 2:14).

I am convinced it will also take a flood from *two directions* to flood the earth with revival and release God's glory in the earth! You already know about the anointing of God that falls *upon* men and women. Let me introduce you to the "fountains of the deep" destined to participate in the second great flood to inundate this planet. Jesus said:

> He that believeth on me, as the scripture hath said, *out of his belly shall flow rivers of living water.*
> —JOHN 7:38, EMPHASIS ADDED

What did Jesus say to the disciples about the Holy Spirit? He said in Acts 1:8: "But ye shall receive power, after that the Holy Ghost is come upon you: and ye shall be witnesses unto me both in Jerusalem, and in all Judaea, and in Samaria, and unto the uttermost part of the earth."

The Greek word for *power* in this verse is *dunamis*. According to *Strong's Exhaustive Concordance of the Bible*, it means, "force, miraculous power, ability, abundance, meaning, might, strength, violence, mighty (wonderful) work."[4]

ARE YOU PREPARED TO LIVE LIFE WITHOUT THE POWER OF THE HOLY SPIRIT?

The English words *dynamic, dynamo* and *dynamite* all come from the same Greek word Jesus used to describe the power we receive from the Holy Spirit. Are you prepared to live life without that power just because some men say God stopped keeping His promises?

What can the baptism in the Holy Spirit do for you? Let Joshua answer that question for you:

> And Joshua said unto the people, Sanctify yourselves: for tomorrow [before you cross over to the land of the promises] *the LORD will do wonders among you.*
>
> —JOSHUA 3:5, EMPHASIS ADDED

An examination of this passage in the original Hebrew reveals that not only did the Lord want to do wonders in the midst of his people, but he also wanted to cause them to *be* a wonder![5] Isaiah said it this way, "Behold, I and the children whom the LORD hath given me are for signs and for wonders in Israel from the LORD of hosts, which dwelleth in mount Zion" (Isa. 8:18).

THE HOLY SPIRIT WILL MAKE YOU A WALKING, TALKING WONDER!

Most of the time we miss God's point. Many of us still believe that if somehow we "pray right" or "do right," then "He might…"

No, God the Holy Spirit is out to do nothing less than make you a wonder, by living inside of your body and showing up in every area of your life! He is going to paint you with a fragrance that attracts His favor and then send you out into a hell-bound generation as a walking, talking wonder!

I am a bona fide, Holy Spirit-filled, fire-baptized, Bible-reading, devil-stomping, sin-eradicating wonder because of Him! I live when I should die. I shout with joy when I should cry. He feeds me with spiritual food that the unredeemed know nothing about. He makes my feet to walk on the high places, and He keeps me from falling with His unseen but almighty hand. I am a wonder of His grace, a wonder of His mercy, a wonder of His majesty and a wonder of His healing power.

Acts 2 describes the first time the Holy Spirit came in power:

> And when the day of Pentecost was fully come, they were all with one accord in one place. And suddenly there came a sound from heaven as *of a rushing mighty wind,* and it filled all the house where they were sitting. And there appeared unto them *cloven tongues like as of fire,* and it *sat upon each of them.* And they were all *filled with the Holy Ghost,* and began to *speak with other tongues,* as the Spirit gave them utterance.
>
> —ACTS 2:1–4, EMPHASIS ADDED

Did you know that there's a "sound of Pentecost"? Most Christians expect their gatherings to be quiet, but that is not the nature of the Spirit of Pentecost! Once the Holy Spirit touches you and endues you with power, you find it nearly impossible to be quiet and still. A parked car is quiet and still, but don't you start the engine and engage the power and then expect that vehicle to remain that way? Power changes things!

I am a bona fide, Holy Spirit-filled, fire-baptized, Bible-reading, devil-stomping, sin-eradicating wonder because of the Holy Spirit!

When Someone possessing all power and authority comes upon you and takes up residence inside you, "quiet stillness" may not be foremost in your mind. This kind of transformation cannot come from some earthly church headquarters. And it won't come simply because some man laid his hands on you.

The baptism of the Holy Spirit comes like fire over the sapphire seal of heaven's gate. It is the extraordinary anointing and power of God Himself, and it comes directly from the Great Baptizer, Jesus Christ. (See John 20:21–23.)

Think about it: That same Spirit that invaded the borrowed tomb of Joseph of Arimethea and raised to life the crucified body of the Prince of God has taken up residence on the inside of your mortal body!

What About Speaking in Tongues

And there appeared unto them *cloven tongues like as of fire,* and it *sat upon each of them.* And they were all *filled with the Holy Ghost,* and began to *speak with other tongues,* as the Spirit gave them utterance.
—Acts 2:3–4, emphasis added

The fires of controversy and the fire of God's convicting power seem to be stirred everywhere the Holy Spirit shows up. When the Holy Spirit sat upon the one hundred twenty believers in the upper room, they were filled with the Holy Spirit, and they began to speak with other tongues. The controversy hit the streets running, and it hasn't stopped since.

When I was in Bible college many years ago, I could still sing pretty well. (That was before I preached so often year after year that it wore out my vocal cords!) Someone from outside of our denomination said, "You're a pretty good preacher, and you can sing, too. We would like you to travel around and preach and sing."

The president of the college told me, "Now, all you have to do is, of course, say that you don't really believe in that 'speaking in tongues' business." That encounter sealed my decision. I could no longer deny my encounter with the Holy Spirit, nor His power in my life. I had no desire to accept that invitation to "preach and sing" if it meant keeping quiet about the Spirit's power in my life.

The baptism in the Holy Spirit is God's chosen method for delivering His divine endowment of power for End-Time ministry!

The great link between the Old and the New Testament prophecies concerning the Holy Spirit shows up in Peter's explanation to the crowds on the day of Pentecost:

> For these are not drunken, as ye suppose, seeing it is but the third hour of the day. But this is that *which was spoken by the prophet Joel.*
>
> —ACTS 2:15–16, EMPHASIS ADDED

The modern religious scorners who choose to join the scoffers of the first century by saying, "These are drunk with new wine…" do so at great cost. The loss to the church in terms of power, gifts and the fruit of the Spirit is beyond calculation. These people are spiritually parched and need a good dunking in the great well of the power of the Holy Spirit.

GIFTS OF INCREDIBLE WORTH
TO THE SUPERNATURAL CHURCH

The apostle Paul lists nine spiritual gifts distributed to believers, which are of incredible worth to the supernatural church:

> Wherefore I give you to understand, that no man speaking by the Spirit of God calleth Jesus accursed: and that no man can say that Jesus is the Lord, *but by the Holy Ghost.* Now there are diversities of *gifts,* but the same Spirit. And there are differences of *administrations,* but the same Lord. And there are diversities of *operations,* but it is the same God which worketh all in all. But the manifestation of the Spirit is given to *every man* to profit withal. For to one is given by the Spirit the *word of*

wisdom; to another the *word of knowledge* by the same Spirit; to another *faith* by the same Spirit; to another the *gifts of healing* by the same Spirit; to another the *working of miracles;* to another *prophecy;* to another *discerning of spirits;* to another *divers kinds of tongues;* to another the interpretation of tongues: But all these worketh that one and the selfsame Spirit, *dividing to every man severally* as he will.
—1 CORINTHIANS 12:3–11, EMPHASIS ADDED

In three short phrases, the apostle described the purpose and function of the three great New Testament listings of the gifts of the Spirit:

- The different *gifts* of the Spirit are listed in 1 Corinthians 12.

- The *administrative* or ruling and equipping gifts of the church are listed in Ephesians 4 where Paul describes the apostle, prophet, evangelist, pastor and teacher.

- The *motivational* gifts, the gifts that are operated by the Holy Spirit out of your natural motivations, are listed in Romans 12.

MARK THEM OUT, CLIP THEM OUT, BLOT THEM OUT—OR SIMPLY RECEIVE THEM

If you embrace the doctrine that these powerful supernatural gifts of the Spirit ceased all operation after the first century, then all of these must be blotted out or clipped out of your Bible. But as for me and my house, we will believe the Word of the Lord from cover to cover. We will serve Him in the fullness of His promises and divine power.

Let me tell you about a few more who felt the same way about the supernatural role of the Holy Spirit. Even after the power of the Holy Spirit seemed to ebb from the first-century church due to sin and the influence of powerful heresies and compromise, the charismatic gifts of the Spirit never completely died out of the church.

In the second century, a revival in the church led by Montanus of Ardabau captured the attention of many Christians who felt that the spiritual fires within the church were burning at too low an ebb. During the peak of the Montanus revival, all the charismatic gifts appeared, including speaking in tongues. Two renowned church fathers, Tertullian and Iraneus, found much in the movement that was favorable, but the church officials in Rome considered the revival a threat to their authority and declared Montanism a heresy.

The *Encyclopedia Britannica* states that *glossolalia* (speaking in tongues) "recurs in Christian revivals of every age, such as among members of the mendicant friars of the thirteenth century, among the Jansenists and early Quakers, the converts of Wesley and Whitefield, the persecuted Protestants of the Covennes and the Irvingites."[6]

THEY STARTED OUT SO WELL—WHAT HAPPENED?

Key leaders and founders of many of the major mainline denominational churches in the United States and the United Kingdom—specifically such luminaries as John Wesley (founder of the Wesleyan and Methodist movements) and

The lifeless, fruitless, powerless church is proof-positive of a church in need of the Spirit of power.

George Whitefield (a Presbyterian)—were personally baptized in the Holy Spirit and witnessed the manifestation of the Spirit in countless ways in their revivals. They started out so well—what happened?

Perhaps we should ask the same thing of Pentecostal leaders today! There are many full-gospel or charismatic churches today in which the baptism of the Holy Spirit is rarely mentioned—and even less often seen!

My friend, it is time to redig this ancient well of power and reclaim this gift that comes directly from the hands of Jesus Christ. He is the Great Baptizer, and He is searching for people willing to lay down their theological arguments. He is searching for those willing to believe His Word exactly as He delivered it and then receive His priceless gift of power as He extends it.

We know the cost of rejecting this precious gift. The lifeless, fruitless, powerless church is proof-positive of a church in need of the Spirit of power. Just in case we have forgotten the benefit of this gift, consider once again the words of the Giver of the Gift:

> But ye shall receive power, after that the Holy Ghost is come upon you: and ye shall be witnesses unto me both in Jerusalem, and in all Judaea, and in Samaria, and unto the uttermost part of the earth.
>
> —Acts 1:8

Hold the Line, or Take New Turf?

Chapter **11**

*How beautiful are the feet of them that preach
the gospel of peace, and bring glad
tidings of good things!*
—ROMANS 10:15

According to Charles Finney, the American lawyer-
atheist who became one of our greatest evangelists,
revival is "the people of God renewing their obedience to God."[1]

How can that be? When most people think of revival, they
think of the souls of the "heathen" being won into the kingdom. But upon closer investigation, the Bible seems to line up
with Brother Finney's view.

> How then shall they call on him in whom they have not
> believed? and how shall they believe in him of whom they
> have not heard? and how shall they hear without a
> preacher? And how shall they preach, except they be sent?
> —ROMANS 10:14–15, EMPHASIS ADDED

177

This Scripture helps explain the troubling vision that confronts me week after week as I travel and preach in American churches and auditoriums. I see fields of souls, white and ready for harvest, but the harvesters chosen for the task have not come out to bring them in.

WHAT ABOUT THE MULTITUDE OF LOST SOULS LEFT OUTSIDE?

While God's workers fill houses of worship that rarely see new converts come to Christ, storm clouds signal the impending end of harvest season for the multitude of lost souls still outside. The divine window of opportunity appears to be rapidly closing as the end times draw near.

"Aren't you being a little pessimistic, Pastor Parsley?" you may ask. If I am, then I am in good company. According to the Bible, Jesus said it Himself two thousand years ago:

> My meat is to do the will of him that sent me, and to *finish* his work. Say not ye, There are yet four months, and then cometh harvest? behold, *I say unto you,* Lift up your eyes, and look on the fields; for they are white already to harvest.
>
> —JOHN 4:34–35, EMPHASIS ADDED

> The harvest truly is plenteous, but the labourers are few; pray ye therefore the Lord of the harvest, that he will send forth labourers into his harvest.
>
> —MATTHEW 9:37–38

In case you are wondering, *this is God's sending season,* and you have been chosen, anointed and appointed to make disciples and reap the harvest for the King. His first choice is for us to go willingly of our own accord. His second option is to send us or *thrust us out* to where the needs are.

God first delivered the Great Commission to the Jewish disciples in Jerusalem. They made a good start after they staggered out of the prayer meeting in the upper room, and the astounding harvest produced the nucleus of the first church. After that, however, only a few of them preached the gospel outside of Jerusalem's city boundaries, and when they did so, they only preached to the Jews.

God corrected the problem in two ways:

1. He raised up Paul, one of the most highly trained Jewish scholars of his day, and He commissioned him to the Gentiles.

2. He permitted persecution to take place in order to drive the Jewish Christians out of Jerusalem and into the rest of the world that needed the gospel.

The same command to go and make disciples of all men still demands a decision in our day! What will we decide? Will we choose the "us-four-and-no-more" approach to church as usual, or will we go, proclaiming the gospel and making disciples in Christ's name?

THE "PRINCE OF PREACHERS" EVANGELIZED FROM HIS PULPIT

Throughout the history of mankind, God has intervened in the affairs of men to ignite revival in the hearts of kings and paupers, merchants and slaves through the power of His Spirit. He has used prophets, pastors and gifted preachers

This is God's sending season, and you have been chosen, anointed and appointed to make disciples and reap the harvest for the King.

such as Charles H. Spurgeon, the "prince of preachers," to conduct fervent and persistent evangelism from both church pulpits and street corners with the gospel of Jesus Christ.

Spurgeon, who died in 1892, preached an average of ten times per week, and often in places far removed from his church pulpit in London. He was ahead of his time in his use of the media as well. Spurgeon's sermons began to appear in print at the close of his first year in London. They continued to appear like clockwork every single month until 1917, twenty-five years after his death. Even then, the only reason the publishing effort stopped was because of the wartime paper shortages during World War I.

The strong anointing and wisdom of this preacher's evangelistic sermons continue to affect hearts more than a hundred years after his death.

Spurgeon's American contemporary, D. L. Moody, managed to preach to more than 100 million people during his forty years of ministry. He reached at least 1.5 million people in London during a four-month period in 1875, long before radio and television regularly produced mass audiences![2]

His Uncle Called Him "Crazy Moody"

D. L. Moody began evangelizing the world at the age of twenty-one, and he preached the gospel with such zeal and boldness that one of his uncles dubbed him "Crazy Moody."

Evidently he didn't lose any of the Spirit's fire with the passing of time. He used to say to other preachers, "The best way to revive a church is to build a fire in the pulpit."[3] I heartily agree! As for the lost and the proud, D. L. Moody didn't use flattering words. He said, "God has nothing to say to the self-righteous. Unless you humble yourself before him in the dust, and confess before him your iniquities and sins, the gates of heaven, which are open only for sinners, saved by grace, must be shut against you forever."[4]

Moody was driven to seek and save the lost. It is said that his favorite question was, "Are you a Christian?" He whispered it to people passing by, to anyone he met in narrow passageways and hallways, while seated beside someone at the dinner table, on a public sidewalk and anywhere else that he found people. He preached with equal zeal whether he was in an abandoned railway depot, a grandiose church or an out-door amphitheater.

D. L. Moody dominated American evangelism in the final third of the nineteenth century, following in the footsteps of Charles Finney. Moody helped start Bible schools, inspire missionaries and personally won thousands of people to Christ. He visited twenty-three states before his failing health forced him to give up a "six-a-day" meeting schedule in Kansas City—only months before his death. His greatest educational legacy is the Moody Bible Institute, which has sent more than six thousand missionaries to foreign fields.[5]

Another bright light named Billy Sunday also abandoned the fame of a prominent professional baseball career to take a ministry position for $84 per month. (He was the first player to run the bases in fourteen seconds, and he also set records for stolen bases.) Known as the "exuberant evangelist," Sunday's thunderous voice could be heard without amplification as he boldly declared, "If you have no joy in your religion, there's a leak in your Christianity somewhere."[6]

More than a hundred million Americans heard Sunday preach the gospel in three hundred crusades conducted over a long career. Often people crowded into specially built wooden tabernacles that held up to twenty thousand people.

With *one million* of his hearers "hitting the sawdust trail" to receive Christ, Sunday became one of the most productive full-time soulwinners in history. He boldly preached against apostasy and called lost sinners to repentance.[7]

GOD MADE AN UNLIKELY CHOICE

Virtually every great evangelist in the modern era—including Spurgeon, Moody, Sunday and another great man of God named Billy Graham—was influenced by a young man born in the eighteenth century, Charles Grandison Finney. Finney lived through both of the Great Awakenings and himself led another, called the "General Awakening," from 1830 to 1840.

Finney was an unlikely choice to become a preacher and a premier soulwinner in the nineteenth century. His dramatic conversion to Christ helped shape the pioneer soulwinning ministry that would forever revolutionize evangelism and revival in the church.

Soulwinning, or active evangelism, as we know it today, was virtually unknown in those days because of the prevailing theology of the day. Finney was an athletic atheist who attended the local Presbyterian Church regularly, and even went to prayer meetings. But on one occasion, some of the saints asked him if would like prayer. Even as a sinner, Finney showed more insight into the Scriptures than these doubting Christians did. He responded, "I suppose I need to be prayed for, for I am conscious that I am a sinner; but I do not see that it will do any good for you to pray for me; for you are continually asking, but you do not receive."[8]

Young Finney the atheist once challenged the pastor of his church saying, "Mr. Gale, you don't believe what you preach; were I in your place, holding the truth you declare, I would ring the church bell, and cry in the streets, 'Fire! Fire!'"[9]

While reading *Blackstone's Law Commentaries* in the course of his law studies, he was struck by the way Blackstone continually referred to the Bible as the final authority for all criminal and civil law. This led him to begin his own study of the Scriptures and triggered a powerful inner struggle.

Finally Finney vowed to "settle the question of my soul's salvation at once, [and] that if it were possible I would make my peace with God."[10] That opportunity came after two days of agonized soul searching during which he could not even cry out or weep because of the depth of his struggle.

Finney said an "inward voice" challenged him with the same words he would use to drive home the gospel message to thousands in the years that followed:

> What are you waiting for? Did you not promise to give your heart to God? What are you trying to do—work out a righteousness of your own? Will you accept it, now, today?[11]

THERE MUST BE AN AWAKENING OF ENERGY

Finney answered, "Yes, I will accept it today, or I will die in the attempt." The lives of hundreds of thousands of people would be directly affected by his bold choice that day. Finney later wrote in his celebrated book *Lectures on Revival:*

> There must be a waking up of energy on the part of Christians, and an outpouring of God's Spirit, or the world will laugh at the church.[12]

Finney was unwilling to stand back and allow sin to devastate the church and society. He said, "A revival of religion is the only possible thing that can wipe away the reproach which covers the church, and restore religion to the place it ought to have in the estimation of the public."[13] When dealing with convicted sinners he stressed the importance of an *immediate response* by repentance and faith for salvation. The prevailing view at the time was a near-fatalistic idea that sinners should wait for God to save them in His own time.

The church of Jesus Christ is a supernatural institution that was not meant to blend in with the fallen world.

One technique first introduced by Finney was the public invitation, or "altar call," so common in modern evangelical church life. "Because of this and other innovative techniques,

Finney has been called 'the Father of modern revivalism' and is generally considered the prototype of American evangelists."[14]

It is claimed that more than a half million people came to Christ through his ministry in an era that had no loud speakers, rapid transportation, large stadiums or electronic media. Some believe Finney's book *Lectures on Revival* has ignited more fires of revival than any other single piece of literature in history, apart from the Bible.[15]

THOSE WHO ADVANCE POSSESS THE LAND AND WIN THE WAR

Finney's ministry highlighted the differences between a bold proclamation of the gospel with direct confrontation and a less forceful presentation with more gradual persuasion. It also points toward an all-important principle of warfare and territorial possession: *Wars are not won by those who merely "hold" their ground. Those who advance possess the land and win the war.*

The church of Jesus Christ is not, has never been and never will be a social club, a political action committee, a fashion center or a cultural playground. It is a supernatural institution that was not meant to blend in with the fallen world. The church is more than it seems—it happens to be the most powerful military organization in all of creation, commissioned and anointed to win souls with weapons of love and the truth of God's Word.

We are not here to get along with Satan and his consorts. We are here to dispossess darkness as soldiers of the kingdom of light and repossess the people in bondage. However, sometimes it seems that nobody has told the church of its charge! Many times we come to church on Sunday, spend an hour singing pretty songs and listening to a "feel-good" sermon, and then we head off to the golf course as if there is no war going on. Maintenance Christianity is little match for aggressive evil!

A PURELY DEFENSIVE STRATEGY

During the American Revolution, two significant events took place at Saratoga, New York that helped to turn the tide of the war. A British force under Major General John Burgoyne launched a bold plan to cut off New England from the other colonies and force an end to the American rebellion.

The United States Congress ordered Major General Horatio Gates to block their progress with the seven thousand soldiers of the Northern Continental Army. He entrenched his American troops at Bemis Heights, only a few miles from Saratoga, as a purely defensive strategy, hoping the English would preemptively attack at a significant cost to their men and resources.

The British attacked six days later, but an aggressive American subordinate to Gates, Major General Benedict Arnold, suggested that he lead a force out of the trenches to meet the oncoming British.

Gates let Arnold lead the smaller force, but then he promptly retreated to his defensive position and refused to reinforce Arnold, who eventually had to pull back. The British won the First Battle of Saratoga and set up their camp one mile closer to their objective.

Gates put all of his resources into holding off the enemy, but he couldn't get rid of them. He continued to lose ground with his defensive and retreating maneuvers. In a matter of weeks, the aggressive British commander made a move to conquer the new American position.

While Gates remained safely in camp, Arnold fearlessly led the well-disciplined American troops and drove the British back with heavy losses. Within ten days, the British forces surrendered to American troops, which encouraged France to join the war. This became a turning point in the Revolutionary War.[16]

THE DEVIL WINS ALL STANDOFFS

If you are not advancing, you are in retreat even if you are standing still. *The devil wins all standoffs.* Don't think you can "just hold off" the devil. Make no plans to merely hold the fort, hold your ground or hold your own.

Dr. Lester Sumrall once came across a witch doctor in the jungles of Central America. The man held a giant frog in his hands, and he had cut himself in a ritual to let his blood flow into the frog's mouth. He mixed alcohol with the blood and then closed the mouth of that frog while he did satanic incantations.

Naturally, Dr. Sumrall confronted the witch doctor. But did he walk up to him and say, "Sir, on the third Sunday of the month we will hold a counseling session on satanic rituals and eating disorders"? Some "modern"

Saying *yes* to the God of revival involves risk because revival requires total abandonment to the purposes of God.

preachers might, but not Dr. Sumrall. Instead, he slapped his hands on each side of that demonized witch doctor's face and said with divine authority, "You foul demon spirit, come out! Come out of him!" The man immediately fell over with a thud and then got up as a born-again disciple of Jesus Christ.

Dr. Sumrall went back to where he was staying in a little jungle hut. There was a small hole cut in the wall for a window with a little piece of material hanging down over it.

He was trying to sleep in the sweltering heat while his perspiration ran onto the bed and stained his pillow. Suddenly, the curtain on the window stood straight out as if in a gale-force wind. He said the air became so cold in the room that he could see his breath begin to crystallize. His bed began to shake so violently that it moved all the way out into the middle of the floor!

That was when he sat up in the bed and shouted, "You foul spirit, I recognize you. I cast you out before; now I cast you out again! Go from this place, in the name of Jesus!"

He told me the bed stopped shaking immediately, the raggedy curtains laid back down against the window, and the sweltering heat returned to the room.

You and I would probably have felt satisfied that the demon had left, but not Dr. Sumrall. What he did next has prophetic significance for where you and I and the church find ourselves right now.

"HEY, DEVIL, GET BACK IN HERE!"

While still in his bed, Dr. Sumrall sat up, looked at the window and shouted, "Hey, Devil, get back in here!"

He said the curtains immediately stuck straight out again, the biting cold air returned to the room with a horrible stench, and the bed began shaking violently. Then Dr. Sumrall said, "Now, Devil, when I came in here, my bed was against that wall. *Now, put it back where it was!*"

He said the bed shook itself back over against the wall and then settled down before the curtains returned to their original position. Then Dr. Sumrall said, "Now, get out of here." [17]

This is what we must understand: *The devil wins all standoffs!* God didn't allow the church to be planted on America's soil just for us to hold back the devil as best we can. We came to this land to make the devil return everything he has stolen!

ARE YOU WILLING TO TAKE THE RISK?

The church in America is used to having everything laid out for them in advance and to taking as little risk as possible. But this is a perfect description of a life without faith.

Saying *yes* to the God of revival involves risk because revival requires total abandonment to the purposes of God. It means we *really* make Jesus Christ *Lord* as well as our *Savior*.

God is calling us to redig the well of revival and evangelism in our churches and communities.

Jesus Christ commanded us to go and make disciples in Jerusalem, in Judea and throughout all of Israel. The first three places He listed represent our hometowns, our home states and our own nation. Who else can do the job? It is up to us to walk out and take the territory in which we live with boldness.

Dare to lay down every fear. Start snatching souls from the flames with supernatural love, burning zeal and unquenchable faith in your Lord.

Revival begins in the church when God's people say *yes*. It only becomes evangelism when God's people put feet to their obedience and take the Good News to their neighbors, families, coworkers, friends and everyone else who will listen.

Charles H. Spurgeon, the great preacher and evangelist, once said, "One sign of a true revival, and indeed, an essential part of it, is *the increased activity of God's laborers.*"[18]

I long to see a whole generation of Finneys, Spurgeons and modern-day Billy Sundays dare to declare the truth of the cross to the lost. This is no job for the faint-hearted or the self-absorbed. It is a job for real men and women of God whose sole credentials are the old rugged cross, the bloodied brow and the pierced hands and feet of their Savior and the empty tomb that declares their eternal hope!

Dare to lay down every fear. Start snatching souls from the flames with supernatural love, burning zeal and unquenchable faith in your Lord. This is the stuff of true revival and nation-changing evangelism. The Word of God says it best: "He that winneth souls is wise" (Prov. 11:30).

You don't need a seminary or college degree to share the gospel—begin with the story of your own encounter with Christ and go from there. Just begin! Redig the well of revival and evangelism in your own life, and leave behind all small plans of "holding your own" against the devil. Go for it all! It will win souls, and it will revitalize your life, refresh your spirit and rejuvenate your heart!

Drink Deep
the Living Water

Chapter **12**

After two days will he revive us: in the
third day he will raise us up, and we
shall live in his sight.
—Hosea 6:2

From the time Adam took his first breath from God the
Father until you just inhaled the breath in your lungs at
this moment, the human race has had to deal with
change. It isn't a new development, but the pace and the mag-
nitude of the change at this time in history is unprecedented!

While most people blindly lower their heads and live life as
if nothing has changed or will ever change again, there is a
remnant, a carefully prepared group of people who dare to
embrace the change. These people set their sails to catch the
wind of the Holy Spirit of God with eagerness.

Change is coming to this world. The prophet Daniel
declared, "And he changeth the times and the seasons" (Dan.
2:21). For some it appears to be merely another time of

sorrow, only packaged in a different way. Others see it as a wind of opportunity to make more profit, win more contests, hammer out more financial packages or acquire and conquer more victims.

However, the holy remnant of God sees it as the Father's vehicle to bring in the great harvest and usher time to its ultimate conclusion. Most of us realize there is no turning back.

This remnant knows where they are going and the name of the One taking them there. Everyone acknowledges the feeling that we are "living on the edge" of something, but the remnant group eagerly anticipates what lies beyond the edge. The time to cross over is past; today is the time to possess the land of promises.

GIDEON'S VALIANT THREE HUNDRED MEN

This minority group is the "third day" version of Gideon's three hundred valiant warriors. Of the group in Gideon's day, the Bible tells us:

> And the LORD said unto Gideon, By the three hundred men that lapped will I save you, and deliver the Midianites into thine hand: and let all the other people go every man unto his place.
> —JUDGES 7:7, EMPHASIS ADDED

In Gideon's day, the remnant knew how to drink of God's goodness while keeping their eyes wide open for every sign of change in the commander's stance or in the enemy's ranks. In our day, they are those who are called and anointed to deliver the church and the unsaved from the "Midianites," or literally, "the people of brawling and contention."[1]

The time to cross over is past; today is the time to possess the land of promises.

Others find themselves stalled at the river of decision, but these members of the remnant troop have made up their minds. This river is to cross. They've longed for this day with everything that is in them. The crossing over into a new millennium is far behind them, and they know deep within that they are already walking in their destiny. They have planted their feet and rooted their hearts in God's divine purposes; they will settle for nothing less than total victory!

REDUG WELLS MAKE HABITATION AND FRUITFULNESS POSSIBLE

One look in their eyes tells you they are neither perplexed nor uncertain—their eyes are on the Author and Finisher of their faith (Heb. 12:2). At His command, they have replaced the ancient landmarks and have redug the wells of their fathers, making habitation and fruitfulness possible.

Where these landmarks and deep wells of spiritual refreshment were removed, buried or filled in by the enemies of God's divine purpose, they have been carefully and reverently restored. Now they have become the foundation and springboard for what lies ahead.

Where the church has been suffering from spiritual dehydration in recent generations, there is now an abundant flow of revelation, visitation and application of the ancient biblical truths. We know success is ours because we have carefully redug the wells of the authority of Scripture, of deliverance from demonic powers, of divine healing and of effectual and fervent prayer. We have cleared out and restored the life-giving flow from the wells of faith, of missions and of holiness unto the Lord. We have uncovered, redug and released the supernatural artesian well of the Holy Spirit in an unholy age and have drunk deeply from the well of revival and evangelism in Christ's name.

Now we press on to dig new wells of obedience in the

purposes of God. We are unmoved and unafraid, even when our attempts to sink new wells in the land of promises produce strife, opposition and accusation. (See Genesis 26:20–21.)

Our eyes are bright with prophetic hope because this is the

This remnant church is no longer content to drink from shallow, polluted cisterns of apostasy and compromise.

Third Day, the day of God's completion, when He Himself will make room for us. We know from biblical precedent that *"we shall be fruitful in the land"* (Gen. 26:22).

We have been careful to redig the ancient wells of our fathers. We have planted seeds and watered them luxuriously from God's wells of inexhaustible supply, and we are destined for success in the day of harvest.

The enemy of our souls and those who follow him have struggled to fill, bury and remove from our memory every well of our heavenly Father, but now the water of life flows from the ancient wells once again.

SOMETHING FAR BETTER FOR THE THIRSTY IN THE THIRD DAY

This remnant church is no longer content to drink from shallow, polluted cisterns of apostasy and compromise. Something far better is available to all who are thirsty in the Third Day.

The water from these once neglected and forgotten wells has became a faithful source of wealth, vitality and supply in a desert land. Through them we are empowered to possess the land of promises on a scale our fathers never possessed or experienced.

The experiences of Gideon's three hundred men contain a powerful picture of the way the remnant church is anointed to bring deliverance today:

> And the three companies blew the trumpets, and brake
> the pitchers, and held the lamps in their left hands, and
> the trumpets in their right hands to blow withal: and
> they cried, The sword of the LORD, and of Gideon.
> —JUDGES 7:20

Now we are dispatched as remnant deliverers and righteous restorers of the breach in a nation of broken foundations, crumbling walls and shattered hearts. We carry God's
treasure in our clay vessels, the light of God's glory in one
hand and the trumpet of unrestrained praise and worship in
the other.

We overcome and conquer with a shout of praise and a
dance of victory to our God. New wells of obedience are
waiting to be uncapped by those with enough faith to believe,
receive and achieve what God says.

IN THE THIRD DAY HE WILL RAISE US UP

We've already crossed the boundary line of the new millennium. Now the remnant church must drink deeply of the
wells of our fathers and follow the King in the order of the
Third Day. The prophet Hosea prophesied long ago:

> Come, and let us return unto the LORD: for he hath torn,
> and he will heal us; he hath smitten, and he will bind us
> up. After two days will he revive us: *in the third day he
> will raise us up, and we shall live in his sight.* Then shall
> we know, if we follow on to know the LORD: his going
> forth is prepared as the morning; and *he shall come unto
> us as the rain, as the latter and former rain unto the earth.*
> —HOSEA 6:1–3, EMPHASIS ADDED

Jesus our Lord also prophesied to His disciples two thousand years ago:

197

Behold, I cast out devils, and I do cures to day and to morrow, and the *third day I shall be perfected.*
—LUKE 13:32, EMPHASIS ADDED

The Son of man shall be betrayed unto the chief priests and unto the scribes, and they shall condemn him to death, and shall deliver him to the Gentiles to mock, and to scourge, and to crucify him: and *the third day he shall rise again.*
—MATTHEW 20:18–19, EMPHASIS ADDED

We have followed the footsteps of our Captain in more ways than we ever expected. Although few have suffered the loss of blood for Christ's sake in this nation, many of the remnant have known the force of mocking words, the scourge of political, economic and societal oppression and the sting of public ridicule. These things don't matter—what does matter is that in this Third Day everything holy is destined to rise again.

In a great reenactment of the drama in Ezekiel's "valley of dry bones," the church of the Third Day is rising up from its grave of complacency and compromise. Bone is adhering to bone once again, leaving behind forever everything that divides and separates. Sinews of love are binding us together again with everlasting strength, and muscles of supernatural power have once again clothed us with the ability to perform the works of righteousness and do battle at God's side. (See Ezekiel 37.)

Your resurrection does not depend on the arm of flesh or the whim of men. When God has decreed a thing, He stakes all that He is on it.

We have crossed over and we are determined to take possession in the land of promises, for the promise is true:

For the seed shall be prosperous; the vine shall give her fruit, and the ground shall give her increase, and the heavens shall give their dew; and *I will cause the remnant of this people to possess all these things.*
—ZECHARIAH 8:12, EMPHASIS ADDED

Many of us lost our way during the long years of wandering. Yet, God was faithful; His Word was true. We follow in Abraham's steps as those determined to seal our faith in God's promises with a divine appointment at the mountain of obedience: "Then *on the third day* Abraham *lifted up his eyes, and saw the place* [Mount Moriah] afar off" (Gen. 22:4, emphasis added).

THERE IS OPPOSITION TO OUR RESURRECTION

We can see it from where we stand. We can see His glory rising in the light of the Third Day, but we also know there is opposition to our resurrection as the remnant church of faith and power. This isn't the first time.

Command therefore that *the sepulchre be made sure until the third day,* lest his disciples come by night, and steal him away, and say unto the people, He is risen from the dead: so the last error shall be worse than the first.
—MATTHEW 27:64, EMPHASIS ADDED

Religious types still fear the Third Day. Modern-day Pharisees still seek a way to seal us in the tomb of our past mistakes and the sepulchers of dead works, empty religion and compromised convictions.

Don't be dismayed if the old guard tries to post sentinels around your life. Your resurrection does not depend on the arm of flesh or the whim of men. When God has decreed a thing, He stakes all that He is on it.

The same power that raised Jesus Christ from the dead is at work in you this very moment (Rom. 8:11). As part of the remnant church of the Third Day, you have a destiny to fulfill and a purpose to complete. Take courage and do not be afraid. No devil in hell or army of men on earth can stop a resurrection in progress!

DOING WHAT IT TAKES TO PLANT A CONSUMING FIRE

It was God who personally endued us with power from on high to reclaim our spiritual inheritance. We heard the call, received the fire and are doing what it takes, but we must cleanse our hearts, anoint our pulpits and plant a consuming fire in our churches.

Here we are in the land of promises with the past behind us and our future before us. Are you willing to go forward from here? Are you prepared to be remade and released into the earth as a remnant believer bearing the power and likeness of the King of glory? Embrace change, and be changed from glory to glory. Return to the wells of our ancient fathers.

Drink deeply of the water that flows from these ancient wells, and rejoice as they become for you perpetual fountains of spiritual rejuvenation!

> Then was our mouth filled with laughter, and our tongue with singing: then said they among the heathen, The LORD hath done great things for them. The LORD hath done great things for us; whereof we are glad. Turn again our captivity, O LORD, as the streams in the south. They that sow in tears shall reap in joy. He that goeth forth and weepeth, bearing precious seed, shall doubtless come again with rejoicing, bringing his sheaves with him.
>
> —PSALM 126:2–6

Notes

Chapter 2

1. W. A. Criswell, *These Issues We Must Face* (Grand Rapids, MI: Zondervan, 1953), 47.
2. William J. Federer, *America's God and Country Encyclopedia of Quotations* (Coppell, TX: Fame, 1996), 540.

Chapter 3

1. Isaac Watts, "When I Survey the Wondrous Cross." Public domain.

Chapter 4

1. T. R. Doraisamy, "John Wesley, Father of Methodism." Retrieved from the Internet November 12, 2002 at www.trac-mcs.org.
2. Winkie Pratney, compiler, *Revival: Principles to Change the World* (Springdale, PA: Whitaker House, 1984), 89–90.
3. Elmer Towns and Douglas Porter, *The Ten Greatest Revivals Ever: From Pentecost to the Present* (Ann Arbor, MI: Vine Books, 2000), 66.
4. Pratney, *Revival,* 73.
5. Ibid., 72–73.
6. Nehemiah Curnack, ed., *The Journal of the Rev. John Wesley A.M.,* vol. 1 (London: Epworth, 1938), 476.
7. Pratney, *Revival,* 91.
8. Ibid., 76.
9. Ibid., 74–76.
10. Towns and Porter, *The Ten Greatest Revivals Ever,* 78–79.
11. Pratney, *Revival,* 79.
12. Ibid., 337; emphasis added.

CHAPTER 5

1. *The Best of E. M. Bounds on Prayer* (New Kensington, PA: Whitaker House, 1997), 185.
2. E. M. Bounds, *The Necessity of Prayer* (Grand Rapids, MI: Baker, 1991), 41.
3. Andrew Murray, *The Prayer Life* (Springdale, PA: Whitaker House, 1981), 42.
4. Lester Sumrall, *Pioneers of Faith* (Tulsa, OK: Harrison House, 1995).
5. I am well aware of the clear teaching of Jesus about the way He cast out demons in His earthly ministry. He responded to accusations by the Pharisees that He was casting out demons "by Beelzebub the prince of the devils" in Matthew 12:25–28 by saying, "Every kingdom divided against itself is brought to desolation; and every city or house divided against itself shall not stand." It is true that Jesus did not and does not cast out demons by invoking the name of Beelzebub, Satan or any other name reserved for darkness. Yet it is also true that God historically often defeats His enemies by ambushing them with glory, so confusing them that they turn on one another. It appears this was the case with this young lady.
6. James Strong, *The New Strong's Exhaustive Concordance of the Bible* (Nashville, TN: Thomas Nelson, 1984), s.v. 5144, *nazar.*
7. E. M. Bounds, *The Weapon of Prayer,* 11.

CHAPTER 6

1. The Word of God says in Jude 8–10: "Likewise also these filthy dreamers defile the flesh, despise dominion, and speak evil of dignities. Yet Michael the archangel, when contending with the devil he disputed about the body of Moses, durst not bring against him a railing accusation, but said, The Lord rebuke thee. But these speak evil of those things which they know not: but what they know naturally, as brute beasts, in those things they corrupt themselves." We don't worship or fear Satan, but we must recognize his evil power enough to resist him only through the name, power and shed blood of Jesus Christ according to God's Word, "It is written..."
2. Kenneth Hagin, *A Commonsense Guide to Fasting* (Tulsa, OK:

Kenneth Hagin Ministries, 1982), 39.
3. The Doxology is a hymn of praise to God: "Praise God, from whom all blessings flow; Praise Him, all creatures here below; Praise Him above, ye heavenly host; Praise Father, Son, and Holy Ghost. Amen." Words by Thomas Ken. Public domain.
4. Hagin, *A Commonsense Guide to Fasting*, 40.
5. Lester Sumrall, *Secrets of Answered Prayer* (Nashville, TN: Thomas Nelson, 1985), 136.

CHAPTER 7

1. W. Garden Blaikie, D.D., LL.D., *The Personal Life of David Livingstone* (Old Tappan, NJ: Fleming H. Revell, 1880).
2. D. Brewer Eddy, *Popular Programs for Meetings: Program One—David Livingstone* (Young People's Society, 1913).
3. This account first appeared in the *New York Herald,* but it also appeared in Stanley's bestseller, *How I Found Livingstone,* published in 1872. Stanley's efforts to find the celebrated missionary won him a gold medal from the Royal Geographical Society the following year. Most significant of all, however, may be the effect Dr. Livingstone had on this adventurer. When he first heard of the missionary's death, Stanley wrote, "May I be selected to succeed him in opening up Africa to the shining light of Christianity!" When Livingstone's body was returned to England for burial at Westminster Abbey, Stanley served as one of the pallbearers, and he later returned to Africa as a missionary just as he said. As cited at web address: http://theatlantic.com/issues// 96sep/congo/hmsbio/html.
4. Lester Sumrall, *Adventuring With Christ* (South Bend, IN: LeSEA Publishing, 1988).
5. As cited at web address: http://www.odci.gov/cia/publications/ factbook/geos/ns.html.
6. As cited at web address: http://encarta.msn.com/find/concise.asp.
7. Ibid.
8. As cited at web address: http://www.datamonitor.com.
9. Ibid.
10. As cited at web address: http://www.odci.gov/cia/publications/ factbook/geos/gm.html.
11. As cited at web address: http://www.odci.gov/cia/publications/ factbook/geos/br.html.

12. As cited at web address: http://www.odci.gov/cia/publications/ factbook/index.html.
13. Ibid.
14. As cited at web address: http://www.interknowledge.com/ russia/rusgaz01.htm.
15. Ibid.
16. As cited at web address: http://www.japan–guide.com.
17. As cited at web address: http://www.odci.gov/cia/publications/ factbook/geos/mx.html.
18. As cited at web address: http://www.odic.gov/cia/publications/ factbook/geos/jm.html.
19. As cited at web address: http://kenya.rcbowen.com/people.
20. As cited at web address: http://www.odci.gov/cia/publications/ factbook/geos/en.html.
21. As cited at web address: http://www.thebahamasguide.com/ facts/population.html.
22. Blaikie, *The Personal Life of David Livingstone.*
23. Mindy Belz, "Memo to Washington," *World Magazine,* March 31, 2001.
24. As cited at web address: http://www.nutritionhighway.com/ sudan.html.

CHAPTER 8

1. *The Astounding Diary of Dr. John G. Lake* (Dallas, TX: Christ for the Nations, 1987), 9.
2. *John G. Lake: His Life, His Sermons, His Boldness of Faith* (Fort Worth, TX: Kenneth Copeland Publications, 1994), 180, emphasis added.
3. *John G. Lake: The Complete Collection of His Life Teachings* (Tulsa, OK: Albury, 1999), 120.
4. *Columbia Encyclopedia,* 20, 34.
5. As cited at www.kathrynkuhlman.com.
6. As cited at www.geocities.com/bettybaxterstory/index2.html.

CHAPTER 9

1. See the following Scripture references: Mark 6:7; Luke 9:1; 10:16; Acts 5:16; 8:7; 16:16–18; 19:12.
2. Lester Sumrall, *Demonology and Deliverance* (South Bend, IN: LeSEA Publishing, 1993), 130.

NOTES

3. Lester Sumrall, *101 Questions and Answers on Demon Powers* (Tulsa, OK: Harrison House, 1983), 64–65.
4. Ibid., 81.
5. Jesus made it clear that demons may try to reenter the body of someone who has been delivered of demonization. (See Matthew 12:43–45.) Those who fill the void left by the demons' departure with the presence of Jesus Christ have nothing to fear. Those who do not may be repossessed, and the delighted demons may bring with them seven additional demons more powerful than themselves, leaving the person in worse shape than they were before the deliverance. Dr. Sumrall shared many of these details with me in personal conversations and public ministry. Additional notes drawn and adapted from *101 Questions and Answers,* pages 64–65 and 80–81.
6. Sumrall, *101 Questions and Answers,* 81.
7. Ibid.
8. "Quotables," *World Magazine,* March 19, 2002, 12.
9. Rod Parsley, *On the Brink: Breaking Through Every Obstacle into the Glory of God* (Nashville, TN: Thomas Nelson, 2000), 131, emphasized in original text.

CHAPTER 10

1. As cited at www.christianword.org/revival/evanroberts.html.
2. Pratney, *Revival,* 191; and Towns and Porter, *The Ten Greatest Revivals Ever,* 31. Various aspects of this report are included in both books.
3. Towns and Porter, *The Ten Greatest Revivals Ever,* 34–41.
4. Strong, *The New Strong's Exhaustive Concordance of the Bible,* s.v. 1410–1411, *dunamis.*
5. Ibid., s.v. 6381, *pala.*
6. Don Basham, *A Handbook on Holy Spirit Baptism* (Springdale, PA: Whitaker House, 1969), 14–15.

CHAPTER 11

1. Towns and Porter, *The Ten Greatest Revivals Ever,* 201.
2. John Woodbridge, ed., *More Than Conquerors* (Chicago: Moody Press, 1992), 195–200.
3. Frank S. Mead, editor and compiler, 12,000 *Religious Quotations* (Grand Rapids, MI: Baker, 1965), 354.

4. Ibid., 239.
5. Woodbridge, *More Than Conquerors*, 140–147.
6. Mead, 12,000 *Religions Quotations,* 259.
7. Woodbridge, *More Than Conquerors*, 152–153.
8. Charles G. Finney, *The Autobiography of Charles G. Finney.* As cited at http://bible.christiansunite.com/Charles_Finney/ finneyol.shtml
9. P. C. Headley, *Evangelists in the Church* (Boston, MA: Hoyt, 1875), 128.
10. Pratney, *Revival,* 129.
11. Ibid., 130.
12. Charles Finney, *Lectures on Revival,* "When Revival Is to Be Expected," (Minneapolis, MN: Bethany House, 1989), 21.
13. Ibid.
14. Towns and Porter, *The Ten Greatest Revivals Ever,* 102.
15. As cited at www.revival-library.org/catalogues/world2/finney-autobiography.
16. As cited at www.patriotresource.com/people/gates.html.
17. Sumrall, *Demonology and Deliverance.*
18. Charles H. Spurgeon, "A Revival Sermon," delivered on Sunday, January 26, 1860.

CHAPTER 12

1. Strong, *The New Strong's Exhaustive Concordance of the Bible,* s.v. 479–480, *Midianites.*

Bibliography

Dowley, Tim, ed. *Eerdmans' Handbook to the History of Christianity.* Carmel, NY: Guidepost, 1977.

Duffeld, Guy P. and Nathaniel M. Van Cleave. *Foundations of Pentecostal Theology.* San Dimas, CA: LIFE Bible College, 1987.

Dunning, H. Ray. *Grace, Faith and Holiness.* Kansas City, MO: Beacon Hill Press, 1988.

Erickson, Millard J. *Christian Theology.* Grand Rapids, MI: Baker Book House, 1985.

———. *Introducing Christian Doctrine.* Grand Rapids, MI: Baker Book House, 1992.

Ewert, David. *A General Introduction to the Bible.* Grand Rapids, MI: Zondervan Publishing House,1983.

Gaebelein, Frank E., gen. ed. *The Expositor's Bible Commentary,* Volume 1-12. Grand Rapids, MI: Zondervan Publishing House, 1981.

Garrett, James Leo. *Systematic Theology: Biblical, Historical, and Evangelical,* Volume 1. Grand Rapids, MI: William B. Eerdmans Publishing Company, 1990.

———. *Systematic Theology: Biblical, Historical, and Evangelical,* Volume 2. Grand Rapids, MI: William B. Eerdmans Publishing Company, 1995.

Hart, Larry D. *Truth Aflame.* Nashville, TN: Thomas Nelson Publishing, 1999.

Heitzenrater, Richard J. *The Elusive Mr. Wesley: John Wesley As Seen by Contemporaries and Biographers.* Nashville, TN: Abingdon Press, 1984.

———. *The Elusive Mr. Wesley: John Wesley His Own Biographer.* Nashville, TN: Abingdon Press, 1984.

McClendon Jr., James William. *Systematic Theology: Doctrine,* Volume II. Nashville, TN: Abingdon Press, 1994.

Noll, Mark A. *A History of Christianity in the United States and Canada.* Grand Rapids, MI: William B. Eerdmans Publishing Company, 1992.

Norwood, Frederick A. *The Story of American Methodism.* Nashville, TN: Abingdon Press, 1974.

Oden, Thomas C. *John Wesley's Spiritual Christianity: A Plain Exposition of His Teaching on Christian Doctrine.* Grand Rapids, MI: Zondervan Publishing House, 1994.

Packer, J. I. *Evangelical Affirmations.* Grand Rapids, MI: Zondervan, 1990.

Sawyer, M. James. *Taxonomic Charts of Theology and Biblical Studies.* Grand Rapids, MI: Zondervan Publishing, 1999.

Schaeffer, Francis A. *The Complete Works of Francis A. Schaeffer: A Christian Worldview,* 5 volumes. Westchester, IL: Crossway Books, 1982.

Shelley, Bruce L. *Church History in Plain Language.* Waco, TX: Word Books, 1982.

Sweitzer, Albert. *The Quest for the Historical Jesus.* New York: Macmillan, 1968.

Synan, Vinson. *In the Latter Days: The Outpouring of the Holy Spirit in the Twentieth Century.* Ann Arbor, MI: Servant Publications, 1984.

Thiessen, Henry C. *Lectures in Systematic Theology,* revised ed. Grand Rapids, MI: William B. Eerdmans Publishing Company, 1979.

Vine, W. E. *Expository Dictionary of the New Testament Words.* London: Oliphants, 1952.

Vos, Howard F. *Exploring Church History.* Nashville, TN: Thomas Nelson Publishers, 1994.

Wiles, Maurice & Mark Santer, eds. *Documents in Early Christian Thought.* Cambridge: Cambridge University Press, 1975.

Wiley, H. Orton. *Christian Theology,* Volume I–III. Kansas City, MO: Beacon Hill Press, 1940.

Williams, Peter W. *America's Religions: Traditions and Cultures.* New York: McMillan Publishers, 1990.

BIBLIOGRAPHY

Williams, J. Rodman. *The Gift of the Holy Spirit Today.* Plainfield, NJ: Logos, 1980.

————. *Renewal Theology: Systematic Theology From a Charismatic Perspective.* Three Volumes in One. Grand Rapids, MI: Zondervan Publishing House, 1996.

OTHER BOOKS BY ROD PARSLEY

The Backside of Calvary
Could It Be?
Daily Breakthrough
The Day Before Eternity
He Came First
No Dry Season (Bestseller)
No More Crumbs (Bestseller)
On the Brink (#1 Bestseller)
Repairers of the Breach

For more information about Breakthrough,
World Harvest Church, World Harvest Bible College,
Harvest Preparatory School, or to receive a product
list of the many books, audio and video tapes by
Rod Parsley, write or call:

Breakthrough
P. O. Box 32932
Columbus, OH 43232-0932
(614) 837-1990 (Office)

World Harvest Bible College
P. O. Box 32901
Columbus, OH 43232-0901
(614) 837-4088
www.worldharvestbiblecollege.org

Harvest Preparatory School
P. O. Box 32903
Columbus, OH 43232-0903
(614) 837-1990
www.harvestprep.org

If you need prayer, Breakthrough Prayer Warriors
are ready to pray with you
24 hours a day, 7 days a week at:
(614) 837-3232

Visit Rod Parsley at his website address:
www.breakthrough.net